T0360622

Absolute Essentials of Project Management

Contemporary organisations proliferate with projects. Managing projects, working with project managers and delivering project excellence have become fundamental skills in the world of business, resulting in an array of approaches, tools and techniques that can bewilder. This shortform text homes in on the absolute essential elements of the field.

With practical insights throughout, the book provides readers with a concise understanding of key concepts, techniques and outcomes such as ownership, execution, success, quality, budgets and risks. Features include abstracts and expert guides to further reading.

Authored by an experienced project and change management practitioner, consultant and educator, this unique resource will be essential reading for students of project management looking to excel in employment.

Paul Roberts is a management and business consultant, specialising and practising in the fields of project and change management.

Absolute Essentials of Business and Economics

Textbooks are an extraordinarily useful tool for students and teachers, as is demonstrated by their continued use in the classroom and online. Successful textbooks run into multiple editions, and in endeavouring to keep up with developments in the field, it can be difficult to avoid increasing length and complexity.

This series of shortform textbooks offers a range of books which zero-in on the absolute essentials. In focusing on only the core elements of each sub-discipline, the books provide a useful alternative or supplement to traditional textbooks.

Titles in this series include:

Absolute Essentials of Digital Marketing
Alan Charlesworth

Absolute Essentials of International Business
Alan Sitkin & Karine Mangion

Absolute Essentials of Project Management
Paul Roberts

Absolute Essentials of Business Behavioural Ethics
Nina Seppala

Absolute Essentials of Corporate Governance
Stephen Bloomfield

Absolute Essentials of Business Ethics
Peter A. Stanwick & Sarah D. Stanwick

For more information about this series, please visit:
www.routledge.com/Absolute-Essentials-of-Business-and-Economics/
book-series/ABSOLUTE

Absolute Essentials of Project Management

Paul Roberts

Routledge
Taylor & Francis Group

LONDON AND NEW YORK

First published 2021
by Routledge
2 Park Square, Milton Park, Abingdon, Oxon OX14 4RN

and by Routledge
52 Vanderbilt Avenue, New York, NY 10017

Routledge is an imprint of the Taylor & Francis Group, an informa business

British Library Cataloguing-in-Publication Data
A catalogue record for this book is available from the British Library

Library of Congress Cataloging-in-Publication Data
A catalog record has been requested for this book

ISBN: 978-0-367-37037-4 (hbk)
ISBN: 978-0-429-34233-2 (ebk)

Typeset in Times New Roman
by codeMantra

To Sarah, Matthew and Ruby, my 'absolute essentials'.
With Love.

Contents

List of figures   viii
List of tables   x
Credit list   xi
About the author   xii

1 Introduction   1

2 Projects and project management   3

3 Project roles and responsibilities   20

4 Defining project success   29

5 Planning quality   39

6 Planning timescales and budgets   51

7 Identifying and managing risks   70

8 Initiating a project   78

9 Keeping a project under control   92

10 Delivering and closing a project   111

11 The absolutely essential 'absolute essentials'   120

Appendix A – Case studies   123
Index   125

Figures

2.1	Project and change lifecycle	5
2.2	Cost and benefit comparison	6
2.3	Balancing costs and benefits	7
2.4	Project stages	9
2.5	Iterative lifecycle	11
2.6	Incremental development	12
2.7	Anticipating the reaction to change	19
3.1	Three key perspectives	21
3.2	Project organisation structure	22
3.3	Tailored management team	27
4.1	Project and change success	30
4.2	Success factors	31
5.1	Product breakdown structure	43
5.2	Product flow diagram	44
5.3	Product description	45
5.4	Product breakdown structure agile example	48
5.5	Product flow diagram agile example	49
6.1	Top-down estimating	54
6.2	Bottom-up estimating	54
6.3	Work distribution	55
6.4	Standard project/product	56
6.5	Simple product flow diagram	57
6.6	Gantt chart	60
6.7	Effort and duration	60
6.8	Activity network	62
6.9	Critical path analysis	63
6.10	Tuning the plan	64
6.11	Project evaluation review technique	65
6.12	Gantt chart agile example	67
6.13	Gantt chart hybrid example	68

7.1	Risk management process	71
7.2	Risk matrix	72
7.3	Scale of likelihood and impact	73
7.4	Risk factor	74
8.1	Project initiation	80
9.1	Control cycle	93
9.2	Project control events	98
9.3	Project forecast report	101
9.4	Project benefit forecast report	102
9.5	Quality review process	105
9.6	Change control process	106
9.7	Scrum/Kanban task board	110
10.1	Project closure and beyond	112

Tables

4.1	Quantified benefits	32
4.2	Summarised costs	33
4.3	Cost/benefit analysis	34
4.4	Discounted cash flow	34
6.1	Estimating sheet	58
6.2	Resource plan	61
6.3	Resource levelling	64
7.1	Risk register	76

Credit list

The following figures and tables are reproduced from *The Economist Guide to Change and Project Management* (3rd Edition) by Paul Roberts, with the kind permission of Profile Books.

- Figures 2.6, 3.3, 5.4, 5.5, 6.11, 6.12, 6.13, 9.1
- Tables 6.1, 6.2, 6.3

PRINCE™ is an acronym for Projects IN Controlled Environments. PRINCE™, PRINCE2™ and PRINCE2 Agile™ are registered trademarks of AXELOS Limited.

About the author

For over 30 years, Paul Roberts has been managing, training and con-
sulting in the field of project and programme management. He has
worked with some of the world's largest and most influential institutions, and some of the smallest, both public and private, helping
individuals and organisations to adopt the practice and benefits of
effective change management.

Paul has been writing for many years and has produced many books
on the subject, some of which are referenced in this publication.

1 Introduction

A first visit to New York is not complete without ascending the Empire State Building. Before arriving at the viewing platform, visitors are treated to an exhibition of memorabilia which includes designs and plans from the 1930s when it was being built. Until one realises how sophisticated techniques were being used almost a century ago, it is easy to think that project management is a very modern undertaking. In point of fact, without it, the construction of 103 storeys in a year and 45 days would have been almost impossible.

Well before the discipline was as widespread as it is today, mankind has been using projects. From the construction of churches, temples, roads and pyramids to the development of today's most complex digital business systems, projects have been the vehicle to build and deliver things. We hear about them in the media, and we use them in our personal and professional lives. In fact, they are so commonplace that we sometimes find ourselves involved in projects without even realising.

A good deal has been written about the management of projects, not least by me. But when all of this wisdom is boiled down to the absolute essentials, most of what is left is good, old-fashioned common sense. That's what lies at the heart of this book: the essence of what effective project management is all about. Without having to scour many other no-doubt excellent works, this small book brings together the most important project management principles and techniques.

Significantly, this is not a book aimed only at Project Managers. The Project Manager is neither the only person involved in the management of the project nor the most important. It takes a leadership and management team to deliver a project successfully. The leader of any project is its Sponsor. This is the person who may have conceived the project, has secured its funding and is held accountable for ensuring that the investment is outweighed by the benefits it promises to deliver. This book also has such people in mind.

In producing a book which, by its own definition, is of a limited size and scope, it has been necessary to omit some related subject matter. Specifically, I have excluded an exposition on the soft skills which may be desirable and useful to those involved in projects. Whilst appreciating its importance, dealing effectively with people is not the exclusive preserve of those who work in and around projects.

The chapters have been arranged to replicate the general order in which a project may be encountered and governed, from first emerging into the world to the point at which it may be closed in order for the intended benefits to accumulate. At the beginning of each chapter is an abstract, and at the end, where relevant, a suggestion for further reading.

2 Projects and project management

Abstract

This chapter allows the reader to understand and recognise the characteristics of work which may benefit from being managed as a project. This ensures that they may understand the difference between a project and 'business as usual' such that an appropriate form and level of governance may be designed and applied. In so doing, the features of a successful outcome are considered from the different perspectives of the project's Sponsor and the Project Manager. The Project Manager will be measured largely on their ability to deliver to time, cost and quality expectations whilst the Sponsor will seek a beneficial outcome. How and when the benefits of a project are measured is considered with respect to both linear and agile (or incremental) approaches to product or service development, and what criteria may be helpful in deciding which approach is most suitable. For those projects which are not purposed to create a financial return, consideration is given to whether their benefits can or should be commercially articulated. The differences between a project, a portfolio and a programme are explored, concluding that they differ in terms of both scale and purpose. The chapter examines the five essential questions which must be answered if the management of a project is to stand the greatest chance of success.

When examined, the features of a project are very different from the nature of 'business as usual'. This can make them risky, and in need of a special form of management.

A Project's characteristics

A project produces a 'deliverable'

A project is a management vehicle for delivering *change*. It provides the means by which to move from one steady 'business-as-usual' (BAU) state to another, from 'A' to 'B' where 'B' is markedly different to (and better than) 'A'. One outcome of a project is a 'defined deliverable', a product which, by its use, enables the new steady state to operate in a better way than before. This deliverable must be of sufficient quality to serve its intended purpose.

A project has a defined end date

If only to regulate the amount of money invested, a project should have a target end date by which the deliverable must have been completed to a certain standard. Furthermore, since a project is intentionally temporary, any delay in its completion means that those who are working on it cannot be released for other work.

A project has a defined budget

Money may be invested in a great many things in order to build the project's deliverable, including people's time, contractors, computer hardware, software licences, building materials, marketing matter and so forth. When added together, this contributes to what will eventually be known as the project's budget. This must be defined and managed.

A project uses a wide range of resources

A project benefits from a variety of people's capabilities, knowledge, skills and experience. They will originate from a wide range of backgrounds, from inside and, quite possibly, outside the organisation. This is markedly different from many people's experience of working in a department where, almost by definition, they are grouped according to their particular knowledge and skills.

People will be involved in peaks and troughs during the project

People will become involved in a project at different times throughout its life. Some, like the Project Manager, may participate fully throughout. Others may be involved in several projects at the same time, or in BAU activity.

A project has a lifecycle

Like this book, a project has a beginning, middle and end, all of which are important for different reasons, all of which can benefit from some

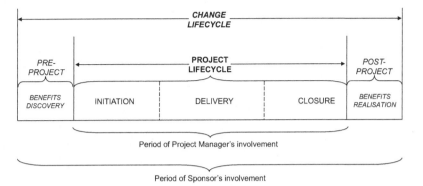

Figure 2.1 Project and change lifecycle.

order and governance. However, the project lifecycle is very different – and shorter – than the lifecycle of the change it is seeking to make happen. Before a project is judged to have begun, time will have been spent considering which opportunities (including projects) deserve the organisation's investment. After the project has completed, the wider organisation should be asking to what extent the benefits were realised. Therefore, these periods 'before' and 'after' the project form part of the lifecycle of the *change* during which we, respectively, seek and realise benefits. The project's Sponsor must be active during these periods, as the time is used to, respectively, determine what benefits may be achieved by the project and to measure the extent to which those benefits were realised. These are also periods when the Project Manager is unassigned to the project, as illustrated in Figure 2.1.

All of these features mean that projects can be risky. For this reason, project management might be seen as a toolkit to address such risks. It is sensible to use only as much governance as a project's level of risk requires. Just as too little management can cause a project to fail, too much can stifle progress.

A *successful* project's characteristics

A Project Manager may characterise 'success' in the following ways:

- meeting the intended timescale;
- meeting the intended budget;
- producing deliverables to the intended standard;

- managing changes in expectations throughout;
- minimising the detrimental effect of risks and issues;
- keeping the team motivated and focused.

However, although this list is well suited as a set of targets for a Project Manager, it may not be sufficient for some other interested parties. Those who have decided to invest in the project will expect it to deliver the step change described earlier. A Project Manager may meet typical 'time, cost, quality' criteria, yet deliver an outcome which fails to justify the amount of money and time invested in the project. The project's Sponsor will be keen to see that the project's management maximises the likelihood that there will be a return on their original investment. Put simply, they'll be expecting *benefits*.

How can projects deliver *benefits*?

How to describe and quantify benefits will be the subject of a later chapter. First, it is important to understand how the comparison of benefits and costs can help to define the scope of the project.

Figure 2.2 shows how a company plans to develop a new computer system which its offices will be required to use in order to gain efficiency savings from consistent and improved working practices.

Into how many projects would you divide the work needed to deliver this outcome?

It could be four, one for each area of work. Or it could be two, one to develop the systems and one to implement across the three offices.

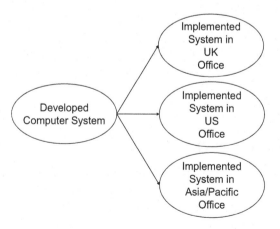

Figure 2.2 Cost and benefit comparison.

Or perhaps there would be economies from treating the whole endeavour as one project. The project's governance and the Project Manager's span of control are directly affected by this decision, so it's tremendously important to track down and speak with the people who have commissioned this piece of work, not least because they may have a very different way of seeing this picture.

One important measure of success for the Sponsor will be the extent to which the investment being made is outweighed by the expected return. Their decision-making should take into account the *benefits* that must result. For example, they might have to consider whether the initiative could remain viable if the Asia Pacific office implementation were to be excluded. The Sponsors will have to ask whether the exclusion of Asia Pacific from the project could so significantly reduce the benefits of the initiative that the investment could no longer be justified. Therefore, the question about how many projects there are can be addressed by taking a commercial perspective, as illustrated in Figure 2.3.

The development work on the left-hand side of the balance mostly generates project costs. The implementation activities on the right, although requiring some investment, will principally contribute to the generation of benefits. If the entire investment is to be justified, it is necessary to know what value may be created from each of the three

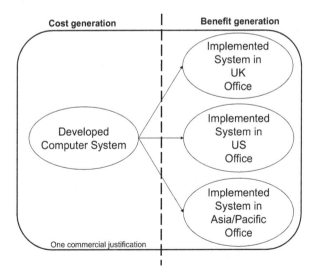

Figure 2.3 Balancing costs and benefits.

implementations. It may be the case that all three are necessary to produce sufficient benefit to outweigh the investment. It follows that all of the work should fall under the same governance so that the likelihood of delivering a beneficial outcome is monitored and maintained. The consequence for the Project Manager of this Sponsor-level decision is that they now have a thoughtfully, *commercially* scoped project, the careful management of which is more likely to lead to what the Sponsor considers to be a successful outcome.

This balance, comparing benefits and costs, is one of the most fundamental foundations of a well-governed project and is described in a written document called a Business Case. However, since the decision to devote a certain budget in expectation of a proposed return has not been taken by the Project Manager, it follows that the project's Sponsor is accountable for determining *why* the project should be promoted.

Should all projects be commercially quantified?

What has been written above rightly assumes that the project in question is being conducted in a commercial environment. However, there are many projects which are carried out in what is commonly described as the third sector within which charities and not-for-profit organisations operate. These institutions seek instead to deliver altruistic outcomes. Many public sector organisations are also less focused on the overt commercial return which a project may realise. For example, a sum of money may be committed to reduce the number of homeless people sleeping on the streets. Is it possible, necessary or appropriate for such a project to be commercially justified? There are several reasons for suggesting that it is.

First, such projects are often in competition with each other to secure scarce funding. A means is necessary for comparing the merits and advantages of one project with another. Such projects may be very different in their nature, but no less emotive or powerful in their ambition. Is it better to invest public or donated money in reducing the number of rough sleepers on our streets, or to increase the palliative care provision available to cancer patients? Without a common measure against which both projects may be compared, it will be difficult for those who sponsor and fund them to make an informed decision as to where their money will provide the greatest possible benefit. It therefore follows that if a monetary value can be associated with the personal, human and societal cost of a person sleeping rough, it may also be possible to know the value of helping them off the streets. This value, ideally expressed in a commercial form, enables one project to be compared to another so that a key piece of information is available to funders when faced with a dilemma as to where their money will have the greatest positive impact.

Second, the knowledge of a project's outcome enables for a more informed discussion about not only *whether* money is to be invested in securing it, but also *how much*. If a target is set to halve the number of rough sleepers on the streets, the debate will naturally turn to how much money is considered reasonable and sufficient enough to achieve that outcome. Having a monetary evaluation of the outcome allows for a continued assessment of whether the funding remains appropriate and proportionate to the benefits.

These are by no means easy or palatable decisions. However, common, comparable values can make the process of decision-making more, or better, informed.

When can projects deliver benefits?

The stages in the management of a project were first identified in Figure 2.1. Figure 2.4 develops them further.

This shows how, when an issue or opportunity has been identified, it may be subjected during an initiation stage to the five questions noted earlier to determine why a project is necessary, who is to lead and manage it, what it must deliver, by when and for how much. Assuming this articulation is accepted, the project moves on to delivery and, eventually, closure. Traditionally, the time after project closure has been considered the period during which the product created by the project may be used, and its benefits realised. However, with a marked increase in the pace of change, sponsors have been less willing to wait for

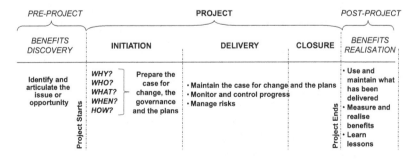

Figure 2.4 Project stages.

months or years for a return on their investment, and users have been keen to use what the project has promised to build for them. This is especially true of software development projects where requirements can change very rapidly and where the benefits of a digital solution are needed promptly.

The development of software has, for many years, followed a 'waterfall' approach where requirements are specified, and a solution is designed, tested, built and deployed. These steps have followed a linear path. In many cases, this continues to be a suitable method for the production of software, and is appropriate for many other projects which have not been tasked with developing a computerised solution. However, the pace of change, the burden of uncertainty and an increasing appetite for digital solutions which address swiftly shifting market demands all demonstrate that a linear approach to the development of products and services is not always appropriate. Critically too, in following a linear timescale, the benefits commonly accrue only after the project has completed.

As a consequence, a more iterative and incremental approach to the development of software has arisen, allowing for the production of features and functions which progressively address the emerging priorities of users in an ever-changing environment. Notably, this allows for the newly developed product or service to be used – and for the resultant benefits to accrue – whilst the project is still underway.

In Figure 2.5, a traditional linear development approach to software development is compared to the method of incremental production and deployment.

As illustrated in Figure 2.6, an iteration is a time-boxed development cycle, usually of two to three weeks, starting with the agreement to a plan which maps out how the resources are to be assigned to the relevant tasks. The scope of the work is defined by a Product Owner, an accountable authority who owns and maintains the Product Backlog, a prioritised list of items which the emerging product must address. As work commences, the product grows in increments, augmenting and refining it from one level of features and functions to the next.

It can be seen that an incremental cycle appears as a miniature manifestation of the linear development lifecycle, allowing for the planning, development, testing and deployment of a new release. Even the learning of lessons is accommodated into the cycle. However, there are some critical steps which do not appear within an iteration, including the cost-justification of the work, the assessment of how many such iterations will be necessary to meet the vision, and a measure of the extent to which the benefits are likely to be realised. Effective project

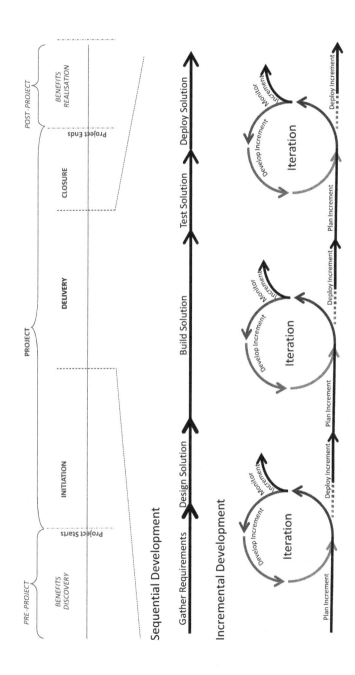

Figure 2.5 Iterative lifecycle.

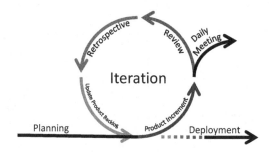

Figure 2.6 Incremental development.

management must encapsulate all of these disciplines. It is vital to recognise that the incremental development of products and services fits within a wider management framework.

The development of software in this way has become known as an 'agile' approach. It may help to consider agile as a state of mind from which several software development methods have emerged. Sponsors and Project Managers should be aware that such methods deliver products and services, whilst the potential for change may only be realised through the effective governance of projects. Thus, a project is a form of management which can accommodate agile product and service development methods, just as it can wrap around a more traditional linear approach, or a combination of both.

In the vast majority of cases, the principles and techniques in this book serve for both the linear and iterative development of whatever products and services the project has been charged to deliver. Insight and detail have been provided in many of the following chapters where iterative development requires a tailored approach.

The agile manifesto[1] has been created to articulate and underpin the iterative, incremental approach to software development. It is composed of four values and twelve principles.

The agile values

These assert:

1 individuals and interactions over processes and tools;
2 working software over comprehensive documentation;
3 customer collaboration over contract negotiation;
4 responding to change over following a plan.

Agile software development principles

These principles serve to underpin the agile software development method:

1   customer satisfaction by early and continuous delivery of valuable software;
2   welcome changing requirements, even in late development;
3   working software is delivered frequently (weeks rather than months);
4   close daily cooperation between business people and developers;
5   projects are built around motivated individuals, who should be trusted;
6   face-to-face conversation is the best form of communication (co-location);
7   working software is the primary measure of progress;
8   sustainable development, able to maintain a constant pace;
9   continuous attention to technical excellence and good design;
10 simplicity—the art of maximising the amount of work not done— is essential;
11 the best architectures, requirements and designs emerge from self-organising teams;
12 the team regularly reflects on how to become more effective, and adjusts accordingly.

The language used in these values and principles suggests that they are intended for the incremental and iterative development of software. However, this does not mean that an agile approach may not be used within a project that has not been tasked to deliver a software solution. Imagine a chain of restaurants has decided to launch a new menu. A traditional approach may drive them to develop and test every dish before seeking to introduce them together on a specified launch date. However, there is an alternative, incremental approach. Customers may be engaged to experience the development, testing and introduction of each dish in turn, so that a portfolio of menu items emerges through iterations.

Each approach has its own benefits and risks. What matters is that an educated, authoritative and accountable project leadership and management team makes an informed decision as to which approach – or combination of approaches – to pursue.

Which approach is suitable?

Imposing an instruction that all projects must follow an identical approach to product or service development creates a constraint which may favour some projects but harm others. Each should be considered according to its unique needs, criticality, risk and relative priority to the sponsoring organisation to determine which is the best method for developing the deliverables it is to produce.

Whichever development approach is to be used, the consequence on the project's management environment must be understood. Here are some criteria to facilitate decision-making:

- Is there an opportunity for a progressive realisation of benefits? Whilst it is not always the case, an incremental approach may allow for the realisation of benefits to commence sooner than otherwise planned as features and functions are delivered during the life of the project.
- Are some or all of the project's deliverables naturally suited to incremental development? As described earlier, software may be decomposed into a collection of usable or operable features or functions, facilitating incremental development and delivery. However, some products or services benefit from a more linear development approach; for example, the procurement and implementation of the hardware infrastructure on which a new computer system may reside.
- Is it likely that requirements will change? Any project management environment must be able to react effectively to change. If the requirements of the project's intended product or service are relatively stable, and the environment is secure, a traditional, linear development approach may be suitable. However, if the project is seeking to meet the needs of a naturally dynamic audience, or where risk and uncertainty are high, an iterative and incremental approach may be more immediately responsive.
- Are participating communities ready, willing and able to work in the prescribed manner? Agile development depends on a close collaboration between users and specialists. Both must be able to commit the necessary time, effort and expertise. A dynamic, agile approach will depend on a continuous engagement of users throughout the development lifecycle, in contrast to peaks of activity at the start and end of a linear development. Whichever approach is chosen, it must be committed to by all participating communities, and adopted both as an approach and as a mindset.

What is a project?

The following definition accommodates the many features described in this chapter:

- A successful project is a temporary management environment created to produce a specified deliverable which, when used, leads to benefits which outweigh the investment made in its development and operation.

A temporary management environment...

A project is a commercial undertaking with a finite lifetime during which a diverse configuration of people and resources is brought together under a common governance framework. When the work is complete, this management environment is no longer needed.

...created to produce a specified deliverable...

The Project Manager is responsible for planning, monitoring and controlling the team's efforts to create a deliverable within the managed constraints of time, budget and quality. The project may deliver a product or service, either in whole or in part, or something less tangible such as an organisation's adoption of new values or behaviours.

...which, when used, leads to benefits which outweigh the investment made in its development and operation.

When used, the deliverables created by the project are expected to release value into the organisation which outweighs the investment that was secured by the Sponsor.

What a project is not...

A portfolio

A portfolio is a list of projects. There may be one or more portfolios within an organisation, characterised by being funded from a common budget or department. It is a group of projects gathered into a governable unit to facilitate their effective coordination and assurance.

Unlike a project and (as will be seen) a programme, a portfolio is more likely to be a stream of continued activity, with older projects completing as new ones are commissioned and initiated.

Typically, the projects within a portfolio are interlinked because of their dependence on shared resources, not because they contribute to a common objective.

A programme

A programme is a management vehicle for progressing, coordinating and implementing one or more strategic objectives. It does so by bringing together projects and BAU activity which, in combination, allow for the delivery of complex change.

Although the terms are often used interchangeably, it is helpful to recognise the differences between a project and programme:

A project:

- will have a single Sponsor;
- will be a contained disaster if it fails;
- seeks to create a deliverable;
- allows for the realisation of benefits after completion;
- has a relatively short lifespan;
- has variable risk;
- seeks to maintain a carefully focused scope;
- typically excludes the management of BAU activity.

A programme:

- may have many sponsors;
- may be a corporate disaster if it fails;
- is intended to address one or more business objectives;
- allows for the phased realisation of benefits;
- has a relatively long lifespan;
- is always high risk;
- will have a wide and often shifting scope;
- commonly includes the management of BAU activity.

What is project management?

Project management is the shared set of values, principles, processes and techniques – the governance – which is used by the project's management and leadership team to deliver a successful project.

This governance addresses five very basic but essential questions which must be understood, documented and agreed by the project's authorities, not merely at the beginning of the project, but throughout its life.

Who *needs to be involved in the management of the project?*

It is likely that a variety of people will have an interest in the project, either because they are seeking to affect it or because they will be affected by it. All are *stakeholders*. It is neither helpful nor necessary to involve them all in its leadership and management. Therefore, it is important to establish the roles, responsibilities and reporting arrangements for those who have been specifically identified to lead, manage and participate in the project throughout its lifetime.

What *must the project deliver?*

The project must produce a 'specified deliverable' such as the 'Developed Computer System' described in Figures 2.2 and 2.3. Of course, this is not all that the project will produce. There will be many other deliverables needed during the project's lifetime, including designs, specifications, reports and many more. Each will be expected to meet a certain standard. All must be identified, specified and captured in the quality section of the Project Plan.

When *must it deliver?*

It is likely that the Sponsor has a delivery date in mind. The Project Manager must understand the importance and relevance of the deadline, whilst taking account of the many obstacles which may stand in the way of achieving it. Throughout the project's lifetime, there will be other milestones which must be met. All must appear in the schedule section of the Project Plan.

How *much must be invested?*

The Sponsor will have a limited budget. The Project Manager must understand the financial constraints and seek to develop a suitable resource plan. The budget which the Project Manager considers to be necessary should be included first at a summary level in the Business Case, and then in more detail in the cost section of the Project Plan, with both documents being subject to full scrutiny and approval.

Why *is this project necessary?*

The Business Case is the documentary vehicle for describing the reasons for pursuing the objectives of the project, and for presenting a compelling justification for investment. It must be created, promoted and maintained by the project's Sponsor who stands accountable for the success or failure of the endeavour.

Project leadership and management

Leading and managing

All projects benefit from a combination of management and leadership. It has been said that management is concerned with the mind, and that leadership has to do with the spirit.

Management organises, plans, co-ordinates and controls the resources to deliver change. As this book is seeking to demonstrate, it is something that can be learned. It follows that managers are often trained, developed and appointed to positions of authority, and exercise their power within controlled structures and defined limits. In doing so, they are encouraged to focus on the delivery of measurable results. Given that projects are highly changeable and risky environments, they can benefit from effective governance.

Leadership can inject the stimulation and drive to change. A leadership capability may remain hidden until provoked, but it must exist before a leader can emerge. Thereafter, experience will drive the development of leadership qualities, possibly allowing the individual to increase their sphere of influence beyond an organisation's typical, structural constraints. In a changing environment, fraught with risk, but laced with opportunity, a community's continued commitment and drive towards a different and better future may only be provided by a leader. For this reason, every project depends as much on its Sponsor as its manager.

Anticipating the reaction to change

A workforce may not always react to the prospect of change in the way that leaders and managers expect. This may depend on a number of factors including the source of the proposed change and its perceived value, as illustrated in Figure 2.7.

Colleagues may act with indifference if a project appears to offer them little, and has been imposed from outside of the organisation. For example, a course of mandatory safety training which is required by law but which staff consider unnecessary may be tolerated at best and resisted at worst. At the opposite end of the scale, a scheme for flexible working may be welcomed with enthusiasm if it has derived from an internal demand and offers the prospect of improved conditions for the workforce. In between these extremes, workers may react with weariness to projects that managers have conceived with little thought to their value, and with caution where great rewards are promised by detached stakeholders who are suspected of having a separate agenda to pursue.

Having anticipated the possible impact of a project on those who may be affected most, the formation of a balanced, representative

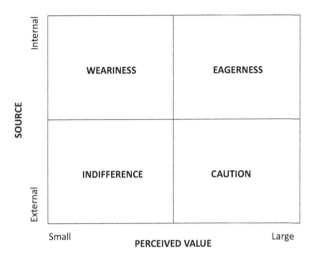

Figure 2.7 Anticipating the reaction to change.

leadership and management team becomes a means by which to mitigate an early risk of opposition from those on whom success may depend. The following chapter will consider how such a team can be established.

Conclusion

A project is a management vehicle for delivering beneficial change. To do so successfully depends in part on the leadership qualities of a Sponsor and the management capabilities of a Project Manager. Even with the best people engaged, a project will face risks as it encounters the unknown. Project management is a combination of principles, techniques and tools which can help to address the challenge of such an undertaking.

Note

1 https://agilemanifesto.org/

Further Reading

Axelos. (2019). *PRINCE2 Agile (4th impression)*. London, United Kingdom: Stationery Office.

3 Project roles and responsibilities

Abstract

This chapter promotes the importance of defining and agreeing roles before making any key decisions, describing the nature and responsibilities of the project's management stakeholders and the importance of their commitment. It describes techniques to identify, prioritise and select stakeholders such that their competing demands may be balanced or managed within the project. The wider management hierarchy is described, including the Portfolio Management Team, the Project Steering Group, the Project Manager, the Project Office and the Workstream Leaders. Focus is given to the design and tailoring of a project organisation structure according to the specific objectives of the project, including a single Project Manager and the accommodation of commercial, user and specialist interests at the senior-most level. This is considered further in light of the use of an agile approach to product or service delivery.

In a project, as in an organised society, people arrange themselves into a community. *The project community can be separated into those who lead and manage it, and those who develop and deliver its products.*

The principles of project organisational design

Although every project may be considered unique for one reason or another, there are some common principles which can be employed to assist in the creation of a suitable project organisation structure.

Principle 1: a project exists within – and contributes to – the environment from which it emerged

Projects are a means to create value or achieve desired change and should not exist in a world independent of the organisation that has commissioned them. Once an overarching business plan has been developed, the organisation needs a management team which can oversee the whole portfolio of projects and which, during the course of the year:

- identifies further opportunities;
- commissions projects;
- prioritises resources;
- secures funding;
- realises benefits.

Principle 2: projects benefit from balanced decision-making

Throughout the life of a project, decisions will be taken which affect its progress. It is helpful if these decisions are taken with the benefit of insight from the different interest groups who have a stake in the project. These groups may be diverse and possibly antagonistic. However, healthy decisions are best made when varied perspectives can be brought to bear on the question. In a project, there are three distinct interests, and it is essential to engage and protect them (Figure 3.1).

There will be people who wish to see the project achieve its *commercial* targets. They may be investors expecting to benefit from the improvements it promises to deliver. There will be those who will inherit and *use* the project's output. For them, its fitness and suitability will matter most. And there will be the *specialists* who build the project's deliverables according to the appropriate policies and procedures.

The project's organisation should accommodate these three very different perspectives in order that the decisions it makes can take account of different points of view.

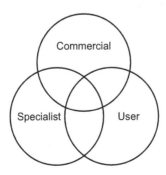

Figure 3.1 Three key perspectives.

Principle 3: every project should have a single project manager

The Project Manager is the single individual who prepares the plan, delegates work to the team and monitors and controls the project's progress.

Principle 4: identify those who are accountable for the project's leadership and management

The project organisation structure must be clearly populated with those who are to be charged with specific leadership or management responsibilities. If they're not to be held accountable, they have no authority. Without a clear line drawn between those who advise and those who manage, the project will be at risk.

A project's hierarchy of management

Figure 3.2 suggests a starting place from which a specific project's organisation structure may be tailored, not least because it is built on the founding principles described earlier. It helps to mitigate some of the more common 'people risks' which the project might otherwise face. The key roles are as follows.

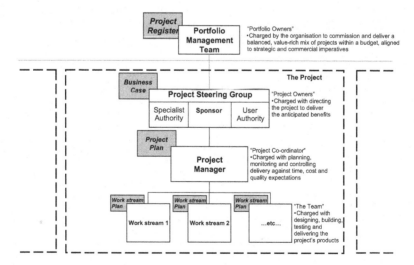

Figure 3.2 Project organisation structure.

The Portfolio Management Team

In preparing for the financial year ahead, the Portfolio Management Team is placed in charge of a range of projects from different sources, including those which have been recently identified and those which are running over from the previous year. It is responsible for commissioning and delivering a value-adding mix of projects within a budget, aligned with the organisation's strategic and commercial imperatives. Thus, the Portfolio Management Team allows for the first principle to be realised: *a project exists within – and contributes to – the environment from which it emerged.*

Commonly, the Portfolio Management Team will meet every month to:

- develop and maintain a pipeline of projects;
- commission Business Cases;
- prioritise the projects within the portfolio;
- allocate resources;
- identify and empower Project Steering Groups;
- manage the risk of benefits becoming unachievable.

The Project Steering Group

A Project Steering Group is responsible for providing leadership and direction, and is specifically accountable for ensuring that the project realises its expectations, commercial and otherwise, as recorded in the Business Case.

Since the project will necessarily become a shared endeavour, it will need to involve many different, and sometimes antagonistic, interests. This is where the second of the key principles described earlier comes into play: *projects benefit from balanced decision-making.* It is helpful to represent the three perspectives in the Project Steering Group, chaired by the project's Sponsor who is charged with specifying and delivering the benefits outlined in the Business Case. The interests of those who will use the end product – the project's customers – are represented by one or more User Authorities. And the essential authoritative input needed to design and develop the solution is provided by one or more Specialist Authorities. This could be a senior member of a key supplier. The specific responsibilities of each participant in the Project Steering Group – and of the group as a whole – are available online.

A Project Steering Group should meet when there are important decisions to be made. However, it is often the case that the participants prefer to have regular, scheduled meetings at which their Project Manager can present the status of, and forecast for, the project. Commonly, this might be every month.

Thus, the Project Steering Group is the most senior and authoritative group within the scope of the project. It will commission the Project Plan from the Project Manager and, assuming it is agreeable to the Project Steering Group, will provide its authorisation for the commencement of the project. It will also authorise any changes to the plan which are so significant as to be outside of the Project Manager's own authority. It secures and assigns resources. It is given its authority by the Portfolio Management Team once the monies and resources have been provisioned.

To work effectively within a Project Steering Group, the participants must be people who:

- are committed to a successful project outcome;
- have decision-making authority;
- can secure resources for the project;
- are experts in their chosen fields.

The Project Manager

The prime responsibility of the Project Manager is to ensure that the project produces the required deliverables to a defined quality-standard within the specified constraints of time and cost. To do this, they must develop and gain approval for a plan, delegate the work, motivate the team, monitor progress and take corrective action if the project faces issues, risks or requests to change.

It is often necessary to make changes during the life of a project. These may increase costs or the time needed to complete the project. It would be wrong to punish the Project Manager for having to breach timescale and budget expectations if such changes were legitimate or necessary. Therefore, it is important that they are selected and recognised for their ability to manage change effectively.

With this important concept in mind, suitable criteria by which to measure and motivate a Project Manager include:

- the presence of an authorised plan, showing progress to date and forecasts for time, cost and quality;
- the presence and use of escalation conditions for time and cost which facilitate the managed intervention of the Project Steering Group;

- the effective and appropriate management and authorisation of changes to scope, timescale, cost and benefits;
- the maintenance of a record of project risks, together with mitigation plans and actions;
- the provision of regular and sufficient progress/forecast reporting.

Workstream Leaders

Those who report to the Project Manager are accountable for designing, building, testing and delivering the project's products, in accordance with the Project Plan. How they are organised may be determined by how the plan itself has been structured. There are two usual alternatives:

- Arranged by department, function or skills area
  Work-streams are designed to reflect the way in which people are arranged in the wider organisation. For example, they may include information technology, human resources, finance and marketing. Suppliers to the project may also be managed as an individual work-stream.
- Arranged by project work package
  Work-streams more closely reflect the nature of the project. For example, the structure may include teams of users, designers, testers, trainers and implementers.

Project Office

A Project Office is often to be found in many organisations that deliver projects. It may perform any of a number of roles in support of one or more projects, or for a portfolio or programme. In consequence, its structure, location and remit will vary enormously dependent on the specific needs of the environment and those who have commissioned it.

Dependent on the scope, risk and criticality of the change, and the needs and experience of the workforce, a Project Office may:

- provide administrative and low-level management support to the Project Manager and their team;
- provide independent assurance to the Project Steering Group that the project's governance remains fit for use;
- support and assure the management of a Portfolio or Programme through the provision of planning, monitoring and reporting services. In this case, it is elevated in both position and name, becoming a Portfolio or Programme Office.

Introducing and operating a Project Office requires investment. Therefore, it must have a clear and approved remit. An outline 'role description' for a Project Office is available online from which it should be possible to tailor something more specific to the needs of a real project, programme, portfolio or organisation.

A tailored management team

In populating this structure, those who are to be held accountable for the project's leadership and management have been identified, satisfying the need to embed principle 4.

Addressing the nature of an agile approach to product or service development, there are several roles to compare and contrast with those described earlier. In Chapter 2, the role of a Product Owner was introduced as the person accountable for the product or service which the project is to develop and deploy. Also noted earlier was the Product Backlog, representing the list of what is to be included in the product as it is developed. The Product Owner is accountable for the creation, prioritisation and maintenance of the backlog, suggesting that, in common with the role of the Project Steering Group's user authority, the Product Owner is ultimately accountable for the quality of the product at each deployment, and when the project eventually closes. This means that they must forge and maintain close and effective working relationships with both the user and specialist communities, ensuring that they work together in pursuit of the features and functions which are of the greatest priority. Crucially, they must have an appreciation of the benefits which will derive from use of the product or service since this will matter above all else to the project's Sponsor. Therefore, in a project where an agile development approach is being applied, the Product Owner has a pivotal role. Given its importance, the role should be represented by a single person who can work as an effective member of the Project Steering Group.

Also noted earlier in this chapter were Workstream Leaders. In a project where the product or service is being developed according to an agile approach, it may be more common to have in place someone to manage each or all incremental cycles. Dependent on which agile method is being applied, this individual may be known as a Scrum Master, Sprint Leader or Iteration Leader. In any case, they are accountable for the planning, monitoring and control of each iteration. It may be seen that their responsibilities are not unlike those of a Project Manager. However, care must be taken not to assume that one role may be able to replace the other. On understanding the particular nature

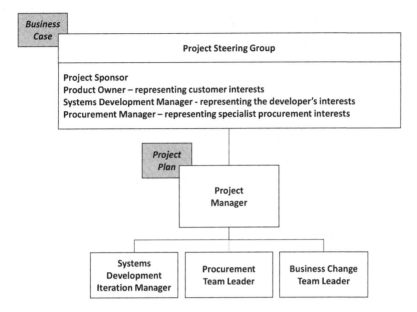

Figure 3.3 Tailored management team.

of any project, it may be determined that it is required to produce a combination of deliverables, some of which may benefit from an agile development approach, and others which may not, such as educated users, new customers or a revised company operating model. Therefore, it is more likely that the manager of an iteration – or iterations – will report into a Project Manager who is accountable for the effective management of the entire project, not merely one part of it. Figure 3.3 imagines a project with a combination of activity spanning iterative software development, procurement and business change.

Conclusion

A robust project organisation structure may be considered the single most important part of the project's governance. It establishes a framework for control and communication. It serves to identify and address differences and misunderstandings. It facilitates delegation and escalation. It contains within it the means to answer any question or challenge that the project may reasonably face. In short, it is one of the first and most fundamental ways of mitigating risks which the project may face from the moment it is conceived. This is good reason alone for considering it as the foundation of the project's management. No sooner is the Project Steering Group in place, each participant may be challenged to describe their expectations for the project.

Further reading

Roberts, Paul. (2020). *Guide to Change and Project Management* (3rd ed.). London, United Kingdom: Profile Books.
Stanford, Naomi. (2015). *Economist Guide to Organisation Design* (2nd ed.). London, United Kingdom: Profile Books.

4 Defining project success

Abstract

Each member of the Project Steering Group will have a different perspective on what constitutes a successful outcome. It is important to identify and describe the benefits of a project in commercial terms so that they may be compared to its cost. There are many techniques for doing so, including a cost/benefit analysis, using net present value to take account of the value of money over time and the internal rate of return to compare one project with another. Other stakeholders, especially the User Authorities and Specialist Authorities, must be engaged to identify their expectations. The Sponsor and Project Manager must broker compromises where needed so that the project has the greatest chance of meeting everyone's hopes. The Business Case is the repository in which these vital expressions are captured. Here, they may serve to illustrate why the project is necessary, what constitutes a successful outcome and to confirm whether or not the project team can disband and the period of change come to a close.

Since they represent diverse communities, the imagined or anticipated success of a project will appear different to each member of the Project Steering Group. Furthermore, one member's successful outcome may seem at odds with another's. The project is the single management vehicle which must meet all of their needs. If this is not challenge enough, different Project Steering Group participants may look for a successful outcome at different points in the lifecycle. Consider Figure 4.1.

The User Authorities and Specialist Authorities may believe that the project can close when the deliverable it has created is ready to be transferred to those who will use it. However, that may not be an adequate measure of success for the project's Sponsor whose interest lies in knowing whether that same deliverable will allow for the investment to be recouped and for the expected rewards to be realised.

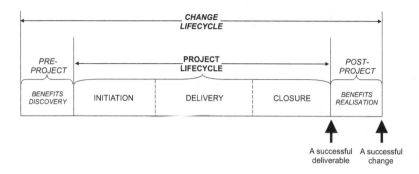

Figure 4.1 Project and change success.

If project management can address these obstacles, there are some significant benefits to be realised:

*   the project management team will gain the organisation's confidence if they are seen to share a clear and common understanding of the expected outcome;
*   the Project Steering Group will be better placed to provide a clearer vision, beyond their instinctive urge to specify success in terms of delivering on time and budget alone;
*   a more robust expression of scope will allow for the production of a Project Plan that delivers what the Project Steering Group *really* wants or needs.

The principles of defining project success

In the previous chapter, the importance was noted of accommodating three important perspectives within the project, particularly in the Project Steering Group: commercial, specialist and user. If there is to be any chance of success, it may begin with the Project Steering Group's articulation of what constitutes a successful outcome, expressed as an authentic set of criteria from each of their respective positions.

Figure 4.2 suggests some broad areas of interest to each of the participants in the Project Steering Group.

Commercial success

The Sponsor will be most interested in matters that are likely to impact the project's commercial or strategic success.

Success Factors		
Specialist	**Commercial**	**User**
• The project approach and outcome comply with specialist regulations and policies	• The project is delivered	• The requirements outlined in the User Requirements Document are met
• Relevant specialist procedures are applied	• On time
• On budget	• Other, expectations may include:
• Specialist procedures, policies and regulations are applied, e.g.:	• Risks are identified and mitigated
• Information Technology (I.T.)	• The benefits are delivered	• The deliverable meets a defined safety standard
• Human resource (H.R.) management	• The benefits outweigh the costs	• It performs to a defined standard
• Legal	• Specific benefits may include:	• There is sufficient opportunity for users to test the deliverable
• The User Requirements Document is sufficiently robust as to allow a Solution Design Document to be created	• Creation of new commercial opportunities	• Users are sufficiently trained
• The adoption of a new 'culture'	• There is a suitable post - project support network in case of failure
• The embedding of new behaviours	

Figure 4.2 Success factors.

For a Sponsor, delivering on time and on budget will be especially important as both factors determine when the benefits are likely to be realised, and by how much they will outweigh the investment. They may also wish to know that certain key risks have been mitigated. Ultimately, they will expect for their project to deliver a product which, through its use, realises benefits which outweigh the cost of its creation and operation. It is likely that a Sponsor may have to wait for a considerable time for this to happen.

Since the Sponsor's measures of success have much to do with the organisation's financial commitment, the project's commercial properties are described by the Sponsor in the Business Case.

Identifying benefits

The benefits of a project are notoriously difficult to articulate and quantify. However, to strike a balance between the benefits of the project and the investment needed to fund it, both must be balanced on equal terms. This means they must be measured in monetary terms.

Typical examples can include:

• compliance with regulatory or legal matters;
• an efficiency improvement;
• the organisation's movement into a new market;
• the reduction or removal of a competitive pressure;

- an increase in customer engagement;
- a project's contribution to one or more strategic objectives.

Taking account of those projects which may not be considered 'commercial endeavours', measures of success may have more to do with altruistic, charitable or humanitarian values. An emotional argument may be highly effective in securing the funding needed to deliver change. However, for reasons first explored in Chapter 2, even these benefits must be quantified so as to place the investment within the context of what it can achieve, and to demonstrate the project's relative value when compared to another.

Quantifying benefits

When a benefit has been identified, it has to be expressed in a form which allows it to be commercially quantified. If this is not possible, it is unlikely that it will make a meaningful contribution to the organisation, or that the contribution can never be effectively valued relative to the money spent pursuing it.

There arc five ways in which a proposed benefit may be quantified, through its contribution to:

- an increase or uptake in revenue;
- a reduction in costs;
- an increase in productivity;
- the mitigation of risk, thereby avoiding cost or expense;
- the enablement of activity elsewhere that will deliver one of the above.

Table 4.1 shows an example of some quantified benefits:

Table 4.1 Quantified benefits

	0	*1*	*2*	*3*	*4*
Increased revenues	**0**	**42,000**	**52,000**	**40,000**	**30,000**
Increased client engagement	0	20,000	15,000	15,000	15,000
New product offering	0	0	15,000	15,000	15,000
Additional clients	0	22,000	22,000	10,000	0
Cost savings	**0**	**40,000**	**10,000**	**10,000**	**10,000**
Reduced headcount	0	30,000	0	0	0
Move to paperless technology	0	10,000	10,000	10,000	10,000
Total	**0**	**82,000**	**62,000**	**50,000**	**40,000**
Cumulative total	**0**	**82,000**	**144,000**	**194,000**	**234,000**

Note: all currency figures denoted as £/€/$.

It is important to be able to express the benefits in commercial terms. In this example, it would be possible to use a survey to measure client engagement at the beginning of the project, and at further points during its lifetime and beyond. If it is assumed that improvements in client engagement result in increased sales, it should be possible to quantify both the scale of improvement and the value of the new sales. When it is time to measure the project's benefits, the intended improvement in client engagement should also have resulted in an accumulation of addition revenues identified in the Business Case.

Of course, it may be argued that the revenue increase came not as a result of the project, but of natural growth in the economy. It follows that if an assertion is to be made in the Business Case, it must be backed up with the strongest possible commercial argument, supported by appropriate measures and audit trails.

Estimating costs

Just as the benefits are an estimate, so too are the costs. These will be refined by the Project Manager when approval has been provided by the Project Steering Group to formally initiate the project. Until then, the Sponsor can only summarise what they consider to be the key areas of investment, as illustrated in Table 4.2.

Comparing the benefits and costs

The cost/benefit analysis is a form which seeks to determine if and when the project's benefits will outweigh its costs.

Table 4.2 Summarised costs

	0	1	2	3	4
People	36,000	20,000	20,000	20,000	16,000
Agency fees	0	5,000	5,000	5,000	5,000
Consulting fees	0	28,000	0	0	0
Communications	0	17,000	0	0	0
Legal fees	0	10,000	0	11,000	0
Accommodation	7,000	0	0	0	0
Other expenses	8,000	0	0	0	0
Total	**51,000**	**80,000**	**25,000**	**36,000**	**21,000**
Cumulative total	**51,000**	**131,000**	**156,000**	**192,000**	**213,000**

Note: all currency figures denoted as £/€/$.

Table 4.3 compares the costs and benefits over five years. It appears to show that the benefits accumulate sufficiently enough as to out-weigh the costs in year 3, when 'payback' is achieved.

The value of money

The example in Table 4.3 takes no account of the changing value of money over time. Future income is worth less than income today, be-cause money received now could be invested. Assuming an interest rate of 3%, £/€/$1 today will be worth £/€/$1.03 in a year's time. Alter-natively, £/€/$1 in a year's time is equivalent to receiving £/€/$0.97 to-day. This means that any value expected of a project in the future must be discounted in the cost/benefit analysis. Therefore, it is important to create a discounted cash flow.

Table 4.4 is a development, showing how the discounted cash flow is calculated

The top four rows are as shown in Table 4.3. The discount factor is the amount by which the net difference between benefit and cost must be multiplied in order to discount it. It is calculated like this.

Table 4.3 Cost/benefit analysis

	0	1	2	3	4
Benefits	0	82,000	62,000	50,000	40,000
Costs	51,000	80,000	25,000	36,000	21,000
Net	**−51,000**	**2,000**	**37,000**	**14,000**	**19,000**
Cumulative	**−51,000**	**−49,000**	**−12,000**	**2,000**	**21,000**

Note: all currency figures denoted as £/€/$.

Table 4.4 Discounted cash flow

	0	1	2	3	4
Benefits	0	82,000	62,000	50,000	40,000
Costs	51,000	80,000	25,000	36,000	21,000
Net	**−51,000**	**2,000**	**37,000**	**14,000**	**19,000**
Cumulative	**−51,000**	**−49,000**	**−12,000**	**2,000**	**21,000**
Discount factor	1.00	0.97	0.94	0.92	0.89
Discount net	−51,000	1,942	34,876	12,812	16,881
Net present value	**−51,000**	**−49,058**	**−14,182**	**−1,370**	**15,511**

Notes:
Some figures have been rounded.
All currency figures denoted as £/€/$.

$$\frac{1}{\left(1+i\right)^n}$$

'i' is the rate and 'n' is the number of years in the future. If a 3% rate is assumed, a forecast for three years hence would look like this:

$$\frac{1}{\left(1+0.03\right)^3} \rightarrow \frac{1}{\left(1.03\right)^3} \rightarrow \frac{1}{\left(1.0609\right)} = 0.94$$

When the discounted net values are accumulated over time, a discounted cash flow emerges. In the example, a Net Present Value (NPV) of £/€/$15,511 is recorded in year 4. Compared to the non-discounted figures, the point at which payback is achieved is now one year later. This realistic expression of the project's projected finances gives a new complexion to the endeavour. The Sponsor should be well aware of this before committing precious resources.

Comparing one project with another

An Internal Rate of Return (IRR) can be used to determine which of a number of projects is commercially more attractive. The IRR is the interest rate which would have been paid on the money borrowed to deliver a break-even project. In the example above, the project yields £/€/$15,511 NPV, assuming a 3% rate. An interest rate of 20% would yield a −£/€/$6,374 NPV. A zero NPV is achieved with a rate that is a little under 14%. This is the IRR.

Generally speaking, a project with a higher IRR is more attractive. However, it is important to know that no account is taken of the size of the project; projects requiring very different levels of investment may have a comparable IRR.

Incremental benefits

A project which delivers benefits incrementally, perhaps employing an agile development approach to do so, remains just as dependent on its Business Case to establish its continued viability. Attractive as the emergence of benefits throughout the project may be, the costs will continue to accrue; both must be reflected in the cost/benefit analysis.

The intense collaborative nature of an agile development lifecycle encourages a close working relationship between users and specialists.

It is important to remember that, whilst this is to be applauded, there is a third perspective at play in the project; the interests of those who are funding it, represented in the form of the project's Sponsor. The Sponsor must continue to maintain an interest in the relative balance between the cost of the project and the rewards it is enabling. Eventually, all projects come to a close. Some time later it must be possible to demonstrate that the investment in it was justifiable.

User success

On behalf of the users, the User Authority is both responsible and accountable for ensuring that whatever the project creates is fit for its intended use. In other words, they have an interest in the quality of the project's output. 'Quality' is the total set of features and characteristics of a product or service which bear on its ability to satisfy stated needs.

A User Requirements Document can serve as a place within which to capture those needs. However, whilst this helpfully focuses attention on the features of the project's deliverable, it may also serve as a diversion from other more subjective measures. For example, it may matter that a post-project support network is put in place when the project's development team has disbanded. If this is only an assumed requirement, it may be forgotten for inclusion in the plan, and remain ultimately undelivered.

Figure 4.2 lists some further examples of equally subjective matters.

Where a project is employing an agile approach to product or service development, the Product Owner should have a position on the project's Steering Group as a user authority, in part accountable for describing and promoting the outcomes expected by those they represent. This may be facilitated by the Product Vision, a component part of the entire project's vision, which describes the intended product's or service's future state. This has its place alongside the Business Case which articulates the value which the project is expected to deliver.

The Product Vision may be supplemented by a Product Roadmap to describe the product's intended development trajectory from its present to future state.

Specialist success

The specialists are those who will design and develop the solution which meets the needs of the users within the Sponsor's commercial parameters. What success looks like to them will depend very much upon which specialism they represent. Amongst others, Figure 4.2 identifies three examples, IT, HR and legal, each of which may require compliance with specific procedures, policies and regulations. If such expectations are not articulated, the Project Manager may remain unaware of them, or unable to develop a plan that meets them.

Achieving clarity and commitment

Without compromise, contradictory or antagonistic expectations will result in confusion for the Project Manager and misleading assumptions about what the project can achieve. The Project Steering Group, led and directed by the Sponsor, must identify contradictions, and agree to compromises so that everyone, including the Project Manager, has a clear and common understanding of what project success looks like. A measure of the Project Steering Group's effectiveness is that it is able to commit to a vision which satisfies each of their respective needs, and which serves as a foundation on which the Project Manager may develop a plan.

A meeting of the Project Steering Group will help to initiate the process of understanding. In preparation, each member may be asked: *how would you describe a successful outcome?* The Sponsor should be especially well briefed since there may be disagreement or confusion amongst participants to be overcome. Mutual understanding of each person's perspectives should be sought. Describing some of the typical differences between their various perspectives can help to identify areas where compromise is necessary. Great care should be taken to have them express their expectations fully. The 'SMART' approach is helpful; seek success criteria which are Specific, Measurable, Achievable, Realistic and Timely.

Each of the three perspectives (commercial, user and specialist) may be taken in turn so that a list to which they can commit may be defined and refined.

Having developed a draft list of success criteria, a further question may be posed: *in what order may these be prioritised?* This encourages a debate amongst the Project Steering Group participants as to what matters most, resulting in a list of roughly prioritised measures. Furthermore, this identifies those lower-ranked expectations which may not be met if time or budget become restricted.

Although often considered to be a purely commercial document, the Business Case is the perfect repository for the entire prioritised list of success criteria. A template is available online.

Conclusion

Those who sponsor projects cannot afford for them to run long enough to find a purpose. Projects need a direction and target which must be articulated by the Project Steering Group at the outset. The skills of an effective Sponsor and Project Manager are essential to help tease out a robust expression of what constitutes a successful outcome for its stakeholders.

Once the outcomes are clearly articulated and commonly understood, it is possible for the Project Manager to develop a Project Plan which shows how success may be achieved.

Further reading

Sheen, Raymond; Gallo, Amy. (2015). *HBR Guide to Building Your Business Case.* Cambridge, MA: Harvard Business School Publishing Corporation.

5 Planning quality

Abstract

It is important to use knowledge of the project's expected success criteria to determine which deliverables are needed. Only when these deliverables have been identified and described is it possible to develop a plan which shows how time and money will be spent. Where a project has chosen to develop its products or services according to an agile approach, quality may be delivered incrementally. In either case, product-based planning is a commonly used technique to define the scope of the project in terms of its deliverables, to show them in a sequence determined by their dependence on each other and to describe each one fully. It can be used to involve the entire team in the process, encouraging commitment to the emerging plan, and can engage the Project Steering Group in discussions about how the project is to be delivered.

It is often the case that a Project Plan will dwell on the journey at the expense of describing the destination. Managers can become obsessed with *process* when they might gain much by focusing on the *products* which the project must create. Some of the consequences of failing to focus on what must be delivered are:

- a false belief that activity equates to progress;
- a tendency to start spending money before it is known what outcome must be achieved;
- a failure to accurately predict the time needed to complete the work;
- a failure to accurately predict the resource requirements;
- greater difficulty in identifying and managing the risks;
- an inability to clearly and commonly define, communicate and understand the quality which is expected.

At the very least, a plan is composed from three key components:

- a time schedule, to show how the available time is to be used;
- a resource or cost plan, to explain how and where the budget will be invested;
- a quality plan, to describe how the project will produce deliverables that meet a sufficient standard.

The last of these three is arguably the more difficult, but there are good reasons for tackling it first, not least because this is consistent with the emphasis on understanding people's expectations as described in the previous chapter. Where the Sponsor sought to understand what constitutes a successful outcome at a project level, so the Project Manager must do the same for each deliverable to be produced. In taking this approach, it is easier to derive a timescale and budget which are more accurately aligned to the required quality. Ultimately, the resultant Project Plan may suggest a project duration and cost which are unpalatable to the Project Steering Group, and the participants have every right to challenge them. However, in any project debate where compromise is necessary, it is critical that all dimensions of the Project Plan are considered. Discussion should focus not only on time and cost but also on what level of quality will be acceptable.

Understanding a product-based approach to planning

For the purposes of clarity, the word 'product' will be used in place of two other terms which are common: milestone and deliverable. Both milestones and deliverables should be products which can be described in a clear and common manner.

If some work is being undertaken that does not contribute to the delivery of an output, it may not be a sensible investment of time or money. All activity should lead to the production of a planned deliverable.

A product is any artefact which is to be created by the project. Examples could include:

- a Business Case;
- a Feasibility Study Report;
- a piece of tested software;
- a communications plan;
- a documented decision;
- a trained user.

The last example is an especially good one to demonstrate the difference between an activity and a product. Training is the activity that delivers a 'trained user' (the product). When planning a project that requires the inclusion of training, it may reasonably be asked how long should be allowed and what is an appropriate investment. To answer these questions, it is necessary to know more about the product itself: the standard expected of the 'trained user' must be defined. If the users have been trained to use a computer system, these are some of the measures which might be used to judge their fitness to do so:

- can they create, complete, amend and save a customer record?
- can they create a bespoke report which lists all new customers within the last three weeks?
- can they explain the process for creating a local back-up of data?
- can they describe the process for deleting a customer record and explain on whose authority such deletions are permitted?

In this way, a quality standard is set which serves to determine how long trainees will need to be educated, and what investment will be needed to have them achieve it.

Thus, in better describing the expectations of a project's products:

- the suitability of estimates for timescale and cost will be improved;
- fewer activities will be left out of the plan;
- more activity will be directed towards producing defined deliverables;
- it can more easily be known when something is 'finished';
- there will be fewer misunderstandings and a reduced need for rework.

Product-based planning is a technique which allows for quality to be sufficiently well considered. The three parts of the technique allow the planner to identify, order and describe the products which the project must deliver. The technique was devised as part of the PRINCE[1] project management methodology. It does not provide an alternative means to planning a timescale and a budget, but ensures that the schedule and resource plan are founded on a robust understanding of what the project must deliver.

The three complementary parts of the technique are:

- the Product Breakdown Structure;
- the Product Flow Diagram;
- the Product Description.

It is highly desirable to involve the emerging project team in the planning process. It not only results in a better and more clearly defined outcome, but also promotes the involvement of senior stakeholders from whom approvals will be needed, and from team members who will be required to estimate the time and cost needed to deliver the project's products. The Project Manager should recap frequently what has been described during the creation of the product-based plan so that everyone has a clear and common understanding. It is sensible to nominate a note-taker because products will be taking shape and some of their characteristics will need to be captured.

The Product Breakdown Structure

This serves as a means of describing the scope of the project by identifying the deliverables it must produce.

At the top of the diagram is the single product that the project has been tasked with creating. This is progressively broken down into smaller and smaller parts from which the main deliverable is formed. These component parts are what the project must produce. It is usual for there to be a debate about what should fall inside and outside the scope of the project. External products – those which are not within the project's scope – may still be identified in order that any dependencies may be known and managed

Figure 5.1 illustrates the Product Breakdown Structure for a project to prepare for and deliver a simple conference.

The products identified here are those which are considered within the remit of the project to deliver. The 'conference' product has been progressively decomposed into smaller and smaller products. What results is an expression of the entire set of building blocks needed to complete the project.

To begin with, the top-level product has been broken into four smaller ones, any of which might be estimated to determine how long and how much money it would take to produce them. However, they have been shown at such a high level that they are not much easier to comprehend than the original from which they were formed. Therefore, each is decomposed further until a set of products emerges which may be understood and described. What began as a single product is now expressed as the sum of its component parts. There are 16 of them in this example – 'Delivered Conference' being one which could not be decomposed any further.

As the plan will be used to delegate and control the delivery of products, they should be subdivided to a point at which they may be

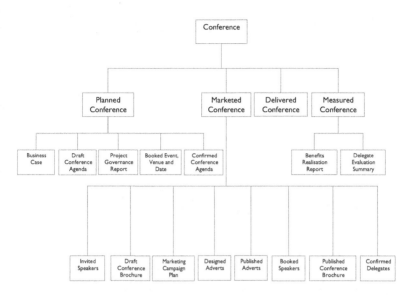

Figure 5.1 Product breakdown structure.

sensibly monitored and controlled. Gerald Weinberg concluded that individuals are most productive when they can work individually on packages of work that last no more than two weeks.

It would be usual for the Project Manager to develop this view of the emerging plan in a workshop with the rest of the team. It is ideal to keep hold of the people who helped develop the Product Breakdown Structure to assist in drafting the Product Flow Diagram. This retains their value for longer and involves them as the plan takes shape.

The Product Flow Diagram

The Product Flow Diagram illustrates the dependencies between the products, and thus the sequence in which they must be produced (Figure 5.2).

The Product Flow Diagram can be developed by placing in sequence of dependency the products which can be broken down no further. It may be helpful to place the start and end products, respectively, at the top and bottom of a sheet of flipchart paper and for the team to determine the order of products in between. When every product has a place in the flow – and any new products have been identified and added – arrows should be used to make explicit what dependencies exist between each product.

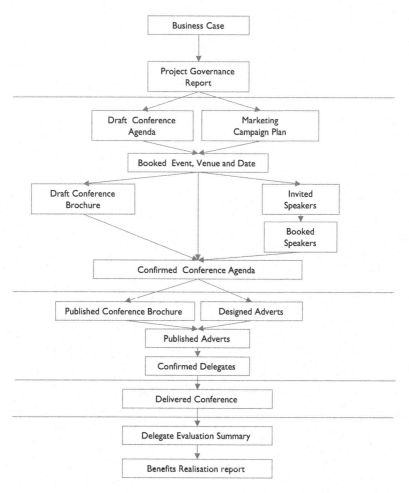

Figure 5.2 Product flow diagram.

The Product Description

It is to be expected that throughout the process to develop both the Product Breakdown Structure and the Product Flow Diagram, there will have been misunderstandings and confusion about what is meant by each product title. For example, a 'Delegate Evaluation Summary' may mean different things to each member of the team. The Product Description allows for each product to be described to a clear and commonly understood standard, as shown in Figure 5.3.

Product Title	Delegate Evaluation Summary
Purpose	To capture and summarise delegates' opinions about the quality of the conference such that improvements may be made

Composition	1. Introduction
	2. Conference Outline
	3. Reaction to speakers
	    a) Speaker engagement style
	    b) Speaker knowledge and authority
	4. Quality of subject matter
	5. Suitability of venue and hospitality
	6. Delegates' improvement suggestions
	7. Summary of actions and plan for next steps

Derivation	Delivered Conference
Format	A4 spiral-bound document, hard back and transparent cover Bearing conference graphics Colour
Audience	Project Steering Group Head of Conference Department Sponsors of future conferences Section 5 shared with venue
Quality Criteria	1. All statements and conclusions are supported by the data 2. It is possible to act on all conclusions 3. Section 5 has been shared with the venue 4. All actions have been attributed to someone accountable 5. The plan is achievable before the next conference
Quality Method	1. Quality review by conference team 2. Section 5 agreed with venue manager 3. Approval by Head of Conference Department

Figure 5.3 Product description.

Title

This should be simple and clear.

Purpose

This section describes why the product is needed.

Composition

This may read like a table of contents. Each component part of the product may be decomposed further if this helps the developer to better understand what is required when creating the product.

Derivation

This allows for the sources to be listed, including the products which immediately precede it in the Product Flow Diagram.

Format

This describes any physical characteristics the product must bear.

Audience

This section lists anyone who will use be exposed to the product. It is helpful to consider this list when determining whether the product can meet its purpose; each member of its audience will have an expectation of what it may achieve.

Quality criteria

Quality criteria are additional statements which determine the product's fitness for purpose. In this respect, they are similar to the measures of success for a project. The product may only be deemed of a suitable quality when it meets fully the expectations listed here. The more sophisticated and elaborate the list of quality criteria, the greater the expectation of the quality of the end product – and the more time and money may need to be invested in its development.

Quality method

This describes how the product is to be tested and may include any or all of the following methods:

* examination;
* formal/informal review;
* inspection;
* demonstration.

The Product Description is the yardstick against which the product is compared to determine its fitness for purpose.

Planning quality in an agile development environment

In an agile development environment, quality planning is eased by having users and specialists participate in close harmony and proximity. In common with a more linear approach, users' expectations must be specified, planned, built, tested and deployed. Here, the difference is that this is mostly achieved in increments. Helpfully, being a method which focuses on a product or service, quality expectations exist from the outset in the form of the Product Vision which captures not only the product's objectives, but also the measurable standard which it must meet. Articulating this is the responsibility of the Product Owner. Thereafter, the product is developed in time-boxed increments and iterations, progressively adding and refining features and functions which must meet user-defined standards of quality, expressed as described above in the form of quality criteria. In listing and prioritising the items for inclusion, the Product Backlog must also make clear what quality expectations each incremental delivery must satisfy. Quality criteria are an ideal way to articulate the fitness for purpose of any deliverable, whether it is produced in increments, or as the end product of a more traditional, linear lifecycle.

An agile development approach may just as readily benefit from quality-centric planning. Figure 5.4 contains a simple product breakdown structure for a computer system which is to be developed in this way.

Whilst the agile approach favours 'working software over comprehensive documentation', evidence of decisions and choices is often best documented. The example includes the Product Vision, the Product Roadmap, the epics (which describe the blocks of requirements) and user stories (which are more detailed needs described from a user's perspective). Each epic might be understood to represent a number of component user stories. However, on the product breakdown structure, they are not represented in hierarchical relationship to each other, but as separate, individual deliverables. In identifying the user stories, the epic does not become a redundant product; both the epic and user stories are deliverables which the project must produce.

The product flow diagram illustrates the dependencies between the deliverables. Figure 5.5 takes account of the iterative approach in the example.

Before commencing a cycle of iterations, this project will first produce a Product Vision and Roadmap. This allows for the identification and development of the epics and user stories from which the backlog is developed. Note how the latter is referred to as an 'updated product backlog', reflecting the fact that it must exist in many states to accommodate the changing needs and priorities of users.

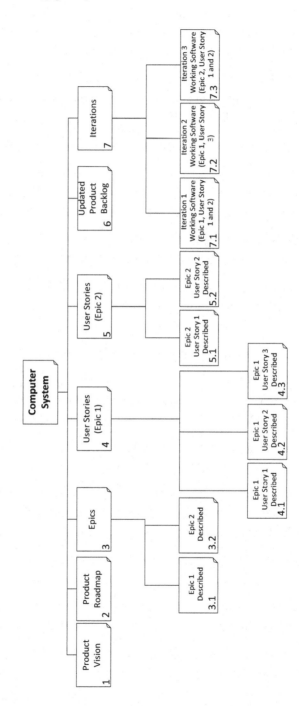

Figure 5.4 Product breakdown structure agile example.

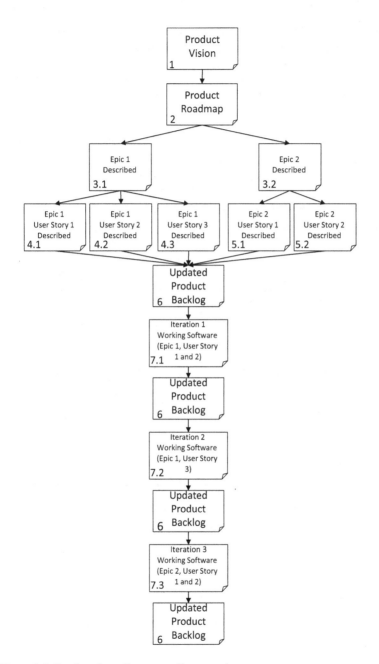

Figure 5.5 Product flow diagram agile example.

Thereafter, each iteration is identified as a deliverable. Strictly speaking, an iteration is a process by which to create a deliverable. In this example, the product of an iteration is some working software which must meet a defined quality standard. If not already contained in the epic, user story or Product Backlog, that quality standard may be articulated as a Product Description.

Conclusion

At the start of a project, when questions about time and money are on everyone's minds, it is easy to think that decisions about quality can wait. However, when the time has run out and the money has been spent, quality will suddenly become of interest. The products the project has delivered will be the only legacy that allows the benefits to be realised. If they are of a substandard quality, those benefits may be forfeited.

A product-based plan places quality at the heart of the project, and serves as a robust foundation upon which to develop a forecast of how long the project will take, and what it will cost.

Note

1 PRINCE™ is an acronym for Projects IN Controlled Environments. PRINCE™ and PRINCE2™ are registered trademarks of AXELOS Limited.

Further reading

Axelos. (2017). *Managing Successful Projects with PRINCE 2* (6th ed.). London, United Kingdom: Stationery Office.

Weinberg, G. (1992). *Quality Software Management: Anticipating Change. Vol. 1: Systems Thinking.* Hoboken, NJ: Wiley.

6 Planning timescales and budgets

Abstract

It is of great benefit for a plan to be well-structured, ideally being composed of products, a timescale and a resource component. It must also be possible to observe different levels of detail, allowing those who are scrutinising it to see what is relevant to them, and providing more insight into the planning horizon which is most immediate. It is easier to estimate the effort and expense needed to develop a product once the quality characteristics of the deliverable are known. With a greater knowledge of the deliverable, it is also possible to determine what tasks will be needed to produce it to the desired standard. Where an incremental approach to development has been chosen, the quality expectations may be realised through an iterative process. However, it is still necessary to establish the time and resource requirements for the entire project. Whilst an estimate is, fundamentally, a guess, there are various techniques which help to inform that guesswork. These may be divided into those which depend on having data from previous projects, and those that do not. Key in arriving at a set of realistic estimates is taking account of people's different rates of productivity. Once a draft plan has been assembled, the critical path – or paths – may be identified in order that it may be adequately resourced and not place the success of the project at risk. When the plan has been sufficiently refined, it may be used to secure the commitment of all stakeholders, particularly the Project Steering Group on whose approval its commencement depends.

Once a set of deliverables has been identified, described and placed in sequence, it becomes easier to determine how much effort and expense must be invested in their development and how long it will take to deliver them.

As described in the previous chapter, there is an important relationship between products and the activities required to create them. Tasks are the activities which result in the delivery of products. The development of many products follows a similar lifecycle. First, they are developed in draft. This draft is reviewed against the Product Description. Amendments are made and the product is offered for approval, whereupon it may be deemed fit for purpose. A sequence of tasks delivers each product on the Product Flow Diagram. For example, the project to develop and run, a conference may begin like this:

- Business Case
  - Draft
  - Review
  - Amend
  - Approve
- Project Governance Report
  - Draft
  - Review
  - Amend
  - Approve (etc.)

These four steps are a good place to start but are by no means perfect for every product. For example, a 'Trained User' might not be drafted, reviewed, amended and approved. Instead, they might attend a course, take an exam and receive their results. Furthermore, if it was suspected that there was a risk of failure, another two tasks might be added into the sequence: retake examination and receive results. In this way, the need to estimate for up to two sittings of the examination would have been accommodated, including the additional cost that this might incur. In this way, the risk of some students needing to take their exam twice has been addressed in the plan (risk management is considered in the next chapter).

Building the plan

It is helpful to plan what one wishes to control. If a Project Manager wishes to observe hourly progress, it follows that the plan must be developed to a level that identifies products or activities which can be measured every hour.

The Project Steering Group will also wish to observe and control progress. To allow the Project Manager sufficient authority to plan and control the detail, the Project Steering Group may be comfortable to see the plan expressed as a series of stages. Practically, this results in two levels of plan being developed: one for the entire project at a very high level, and the other a more detailed plan that focuses only on the next stage. Whilst the overall Project Plan contains less detail (and thus more risk), the next stage plan is developed to a lower level of detail for only the next planning horizon (maybe four to five weeks) and is less risky. As each stage delivers its planned deliverables, greater confidence may be gained in the overall Project Plan. At the junction between one stage and another, the Project Manager may present the Project Steering Group with an increasingly reliable plan. This offers the Project Steering Group the opportunity to assess the project's continued viability before it continues.

Both of these basic principles – plan what you wish to control, and divide the project into stages – underpin and facilitate the use of many of the most common estimating techniques.

Estimating

An estimate is a probability assessment based on skill and experience of the time and resources required for the successful delivery of a specified product. It may also be described as an educated or informed guess.

There are many techniques which can improve the quality of an estimate. Certainly, a Product Description can clarify what is to be produced, making it easier to establish what time and effort are required to deliver it. Broadly, these techniques fall into two categories:

- those which may be used without reference to any stored data or prior experience:
  - top-down and bottom-up;
  - the Delphi technique.
- those which depend on data from previous projects:
  - work distribution;
  - standard project/product.

Top-down and bottom-up

A top-down estimate is commonly used at the beginning of a project to calculate its duration, cost and quality expectations. As the name suggests, it allows for the project to be observed from a high level, broken into no more detail than its stages. Figure 6.1 contains an example.

Figure 6.1 Top-down estimating.

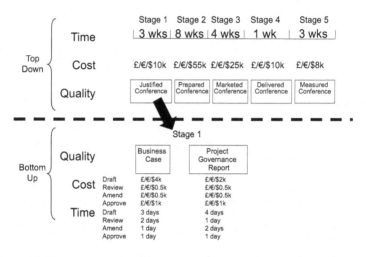

Figure 6.2 Bottom-up estimating.

Although this contains estimates for time, cost and quality, the Project Steering Group will require a lower level of plan which provides the detail for the next planning horizon, as shown in Figure 6.2.

In this example, the first stage of the project has been described in greater detail, clearly identifying that a Business Case and Project Governance Report are required. The high-level information in the top-down estimate is now shown in more detail. This is an example of bottom-up estimating, a technique which is facilitated by the existence of a product-based plan and a project which is divided into stages. Just as one stage is ending, the next is planned. As more becomes known about the project, the level of risk reduces. Thus, the amount of contingency required can be reduced progressively.

These two techniques allow planning to take place at both project and stage levels, and address the fact that the further into the future one looks, the more uncertain it becomes.

The Delphi technique

Named after the Oracle of Delphi, which the Greeks consulted before all major undertakings, this technique gradually reveals a range of emerging estimates to a panel of experts in the expectation that a consensus may be achieved.

The experts who were engaged to develop the Product Descriptions may be asked to estimate the time, effort or budget needed to build, test and approve the products themselves. Their anonymous replies are shared, and the experts are given an opportunity to refine their estimates. This may lead to an agreement. If not, an average may be sought.

Work distribution

While some projects are unique, many use a common method for delivery. For example, a housebuilder will follow a repeatable process, and software developers regularly apply a standard lifecycle to the development of computer systems. Using metrics gathered from previous projects, the work distribution technique allows for the apportionment of time, budget or effort across the project lifecycle, as illustrated in Figure 6.3.

The model may be used in a number of ways. For example, if the project has been allocated a budget, it may be distributed according to the proportions so as to determine the allocation for each stage. Alternatively, if budget has already been invested to complete the first stage, the proportions required for future stages may be estimated.

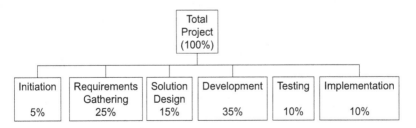

Figure 6.3 Work distribution.

Standard project/product

This technique also depends on data harvested from previous projects. As noted earlier, it is not uncommon to carry out projects which follow a similar process. It is also quite common for projects to create almost identical products which vary only in size or complexity. For example, all Conference Agendas may be similar in construction but vary in accordance with the duration of the conference and the number of speakers. A table, like that shown in Figure 6.4, can be constructed to determine the effort needed to deliver such a project or product, simply by observing its relative size and complexity.

Taking account of productivity

When estimating, it is crucial to take account of the different pace at which people work, and how productively they use their time.

- People are never 100% productive. Like machines, people have times when they are less able, or unable, to produce anything. This may include periods of sickness, training and vacations. Standard productivity, if any such thing exists, can vary between 65% and 80%, dependent on what activities an organisation determines to be 'non-productive'.
- Allocating more people to a task may not improve productivity. Often, the reverse is true, as a simple job becomes more complex for having to set aside time and effort for its management.
- Productivity varies from one person to the next. When estimating, it is best to have some idea of who will undertake the task. In this way, their rate of productivity – including those periods when they may be unavailable – may be taken into account.
- Productivity increases are usually temporary. Frederick Herzberg, an American psychologist, showed that a person's productivity

Size \ Complexity	Low	Medium	High
Small	1	5	7
Medium	5	7	11
Large	7	11	20

Figure 6.4 Standard project/product.

improvement arising from a pay increase lasted for only a relatively short time.

Increasing the likelihood that estimates are reliable.

Taking account of the above, there are several ways in which an estimate may become more trustworthy.

- Let people estimate their own work. No-one is better placed to know how productive an individual may be than the person themselves. They understand their diary, their motivation to work (or not to work!) and, ideally, the subject areas about which they are considered capable. There is also the added advantage that if someone estimates their own work, it is less likely that they can blame someone else for not having been able to complete it.
- Make planning assumptions clear. If these remain unrecorded, it may never be possible to know how a duration or budget was calculated.
- Agree Product Descriptions. As the product must satisfy its intended audience, it follows that it should be commonly understood before development begins.
- Understand a person's track record. If a team member or a supplier has persistently failed to deliver to plan in the past, it may be helpful to add some contingency to their estimates.
- Find ways to motivate people. Penalties and rewards often provide the encouragement to deliver according to plan.

Recording and summarising estimates.

A means is needed to summarise estimates into a series of views which can be scrutinised, refined and approved.

Here is a simple example project which consists of only four deliverables (Figure 6.5).

Figure 6.5 Simple product flow diagram.

Table 6.1 Estimating sheet

	Activity	*Resources*	*Effort/ cost*	*Assumptions*
Presentation template	Develop	PR	0.8	PR committed same effort on previous, similar project
	Review	ST/MW	0.5/0.5	Constrained as slot for teleconference is booked
	Amend	PR	0.25	PR committed same effort on previous, similar project
	Approve	PSG	0.1	Assuming PSG will approve via email
Gathered data	Develop	AK	0.5	Based on 0.1 per item x 4 items, plus contingency of 0.1
	Review	PR/MW	0.1/0.1	Estimate based on MW experience
	Amend	AK	0.25	Assuming approximately half of product to be reworked
	Approve	PSG	0.1	Assuming PSG will approve via email
Feasibility report	Develop	PR	0.8	PR committed same effort on previous, similar project
	Review	ST/MW	0.5/0.5	Constrained as slot for teleconference is booked
	Amend	PR	0.25	Assuming approximately quarter of product to be reworked
	Approve	PSG	0.1	Assuming PSG will approve via email
Compiled presentation	Develop	AK	0.8	AK estimate based on experience
		Train fare	£/€/$100	To visit London office
	Review	ST/MW	0.25/0.25	ST estimate based on experience
	Amend	AK	0.25	Assuming approximately quarter of product to be reworked
	Approve	PSG	0.1	Assuming PSG will approve via email

Each product's duration and cost are estimated, with the results being recorded in an 'Estimating Sheet', as shown in Table 6.1.

The estimates are captured against each task. The third column allows for the recording of what resources will be needed. All committed resources must be included; the example mostly shows people who have been engaged, although the cost of some planned travel has also been recorded.

The fourth column (identifying the planned costs) is a mixture of the effort planned for each person and any intended financial outlay such as the £/€/$100 train ticket. The Project Steering Group will expect a plan which makes clear what budget is being requested. Therefore, these two expressions will need to be combined into one single financial figure. The Project Manager can only provide this when the Resource Plan is completed. Before then, the duration of each task must be calculated. This is only possible with knowledge of each product, and the estimated effort needed to complete them.

Note that there is a difference between 'effort' and 'duration'. In the example, effort is measured in 'person-days'. This assumes that one person could work at full productivity, which we know to be unlikely. If productivity is assumed to be 80%, a duration of five days would be needed for a task which requires an effort of four person-days (on the assumption that they are available exclusively to the project). Of course, it is possible to distribute work across a number of people; a task with an estimated effort of four person-days need not be delivered by one person alone. Therefore, duration can be understood as a period of time, measured in hours or days, which may be shortened if the effort is shared, or augmented if the resource is reduced.

The final column records the assumptions used when estimating the effort.

With this information to hand, it is possible to create a time schedule. A common format is the Gantt chart, first developed by Henry L. Gantt in 1910. A simple Gantt chart based on the information contained in the Estimating Sheet is shown in Figure 6.6.

The Gantt chart is composed from information gleaned from the Product Flow Diagram and the Estimating Sheet. Notably, the dependencies from the Product Flow Diagram are represented by arrows linking products in the Gantt chart. The X axis allows for the duration of products and tasks to be expressed.

In Figure 6.7, attention is focused on the end of this project. A duration of two days has been planned for the development of the Compiled Presentation, although the person assigned to the task (denoted AK) is only required to devote 0.8 person-days to the task (as identified in the Estimating Sheet). This duration takes account of AK's rate of productivity and any other tasks they may be undertaking.

Whilst it has been essential to have an estimate of the effort required to complete a task, the format of a Gantt chart is not suited to summarise the project's costs. In order to determine the cost of the project, it is necessary to have a 'day rate' for each person involved which, when multiplied by the number of person-days, allows for a forecast cost to

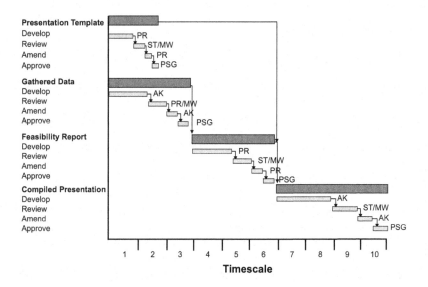

Figure 6.6 Gantt chart.

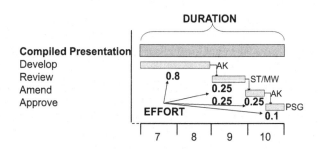

Figure 6.7 Effort and duration.

be calculated. Table 6.2 shows a spreadsheet which identifies the effort and calculated financial cost of each person involved in the project, together with the expense of a train ticket, the only non-human expense in this example.

Often, there are 'capital' costs, such as a building or a piece of computer hardware. This too should be included in the Resource Plan as a separate line item to differentiate it from revenue investments.

Table 6.2 Resource plan

	1	2	3	4	5	6	7	8	9	10	Total
PR	0.8	0.35		0.8		0.25					2.2
£/€/$300/d	£/€/$240	£/€/$105		£/€/$240		£/€/$75					£/€/$660
ST		0.5			0.5				0.25		1.25
£/€/$200/d		£/€/$100			£/€/$100				£/€/$50		£/€/$250
MW		0.6			0.5				0.25		1.35
£/€/$200/d		£/€/$120			£/€/$100				£/€/$50		£/€/$270
AK	0.5	0.5	0.25				0.8			0.25	2.3
£/€/$200/d	£/€/$100	£/€/$100	£/€/$50				£/€/$160			£/€/$50	£/€/$460
PSG		0.1	0.1			0.1				0.1	0.4
£/€/$400/d		£/€/$40	£/€/$40			£/€/$40				£/€/$40	£/€/$160
Total Human	**1.3**	**2.05**	**0.35**	**0.8**	**1.0**	**0.35**	**0.8**		**0.5**	**0.35**	**7.5**
	£/€/$340	**£/€/$465**	**£/€/$90**	**£/€/$240**	**£/€/$200**	**£/€/$115**	**£/€/$160**		**£/€/$100**	**£/€/$90**	**£/€/$1,800**
Travel							£/€/$100				$100
Total	**£/€/$340**	**£/€/$465**	**£/€/$90**	**£/€/$240**	**£/€/$200**	**£/€/$115**	**£/€/$260**		**£/€/$100**	**£/€/$90**	**£/€/$1,900**

Refining the plan

The plan has been formed around three core expressions:

- quality (the product descriptions);
- cost (the resource plan);
- timescale (the Gantt chart).

There are further refinements which can be made to improve its reliability and usefulness.

The activity network

There is flexibility in the plan. It is possible to amend the duration, start and end dates of some tasks. It is also possible to change the number of people assigned to a task, or to reduce or increase a product's quality. However, a change to one part of the plan is rarely possible without affecting something else. The Activity Network illustrates this point. Figure 6.8 summarises the Gantt chart seen earlier.

For a limited period, the Presentation Template can be delayed without affecting the end date of the project. If it drifts beyond day 6, the development of the Compiled Presentation will be affected: it has a dependency on product 1 and will slip by the same amount. However, until or unless that happens, its flexibility may be useful.

The Activity Network allows the Project Manager to identify those tasks and products – like the Presentation Template – where there is potential for movement. Importantly, it also identifies where there is none. The relevant figures from the example are used in Figure 6.9.

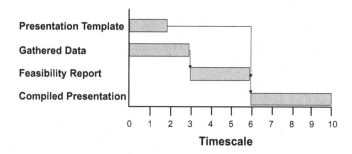

Figure 6.8 Activity network.

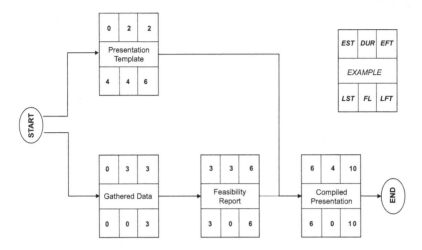

Figure 6.9 Critical path analysis.

- EST: earliest start time. This is the earliest point at which the task or product may start;
- EFT: earliest finish time: This is the earliest point at which the task or product may finish;
- LST: latest start time. This is the latest point at which the task or product may start before affecting any which succeed it;
- LFT: latest finish time. The latest point at which the task or product may be finished before affecting any which succeed it;
- DUR: duration. This is the number of working days between the EST and the EFT, or the LST and LFT;
- FL: float. This is the difference between the EST and the LST or the EFT and the LFT. This is the amount by which the task or product may move before affecting any which succeed it.

In the example, the Presentation Template has a float of four, meaning it has some leeway to move in the plan without affecting the project's end date. All the other products have no float. By definition, all of the products except the Presentation Template are on what is called the critical path. This means that any delay of these tasks or products will result in an identical slippage in the project's end date. Any number of critical paths may be observed in a project. If float is consumed, a new critical path may open up. It follows that the critical path (or paths) is an area of possible risk to the project.

Float can be helpful in that it provides the Project Manager with some flexibility in how the plan is formed. For example, it seems possible to delay the development of the Presentation Template until day 4, as shown in Figure 6.10.

There is no apparent effect on the project's end date. However, timescale and quality are not the only parts of the plan. The impact of this slippage on the resource plan must be understood. Table 6.3 shows how the resource plan has been impaired. The person denoted as PR

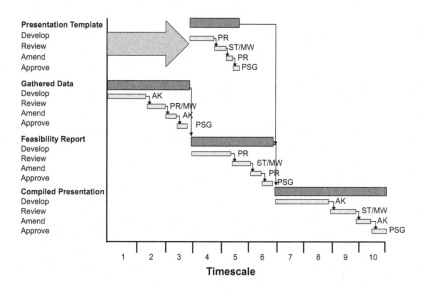

Figure 6.10 Tuning the plan.

Table 6.3 Resource levelling

	1	2	3	4	5	6	7	8	9	10	Total
PR	*0.8*	*0.35*		(1.6)	0.35	0.25					**2.2**
ST		0.5			0.5				0.25		**1.25**
MW		0.6			0.5				0.25		**1.35**
AK	0.5	0.5	0.25				0.8			0.25	2.3
PSG		0.1	0.1			0.1				0.1	**0.4**
Total	**0.5**	**1.7**	**0.35**	**1.6**	**1.35**	**0.35**	**0.8**		**0.5**	**0.35**	7.5

is now required to work on both the Presentation Template and the Feasibility Report at the same time, resulting in an over-commitment on day 4. Unless something can be done, the project will slip, or the quality of the Presentation Template may suffer as PR struggles to meet the deadline.

Resource levelling

Resource Levelling is a technique which the Project Manager can use to smooth out such inconsistencies and use people's time more efficiently.

The Resource Plan in this table contains an example of a resourcing peak (circled) created by the movement of the Presentation Template. This effort required by PR exceeds their capacity to deliver it. However, there are also examples where people appear to be undercapacity. This may be because they have time on their hands. Alternatively, they may be engaged in other projects, unknown to the Project Manager. However, if people have been assigned full-time to the project, moving tasks or products in this way can be helpful, allowing the Project Manager to reduce peaks, fill troughs and make most efficient use of precious resources.

Project evaluation and review technique

This technique was created in the 1950s by the US Department of Defence to assist in determining the duration of a project and in identifying the critical path. The example illustrated in Figure 6.6 may be represented as shown in Figure 6.11.

The products – or milestones, as the technique calls them – are represented as circles (numbered in tens so as to allow for the insertion of others, if necessary). An additional circle (denoted as 50 in this

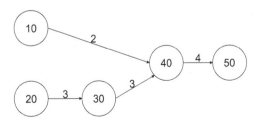

Figure 6.11 Project evaluation review technique.

diagram) represents the end of the project and is not suggestive of a product. Duration is indicated by the lines which connect the circles.

Importantly, the technique may be used as an alternative to some of the methods described in this section, but it has some limitations. It contains none of the underlying quality definitions contained in the Product Description. Furthermore, the technique may be used to determine a timeline, but not a budget. This is because no effort is recorded from which to calculate a cost.

Planning for incremental delivery

Within a plan, time, cost and quality are closely related; if any one is to be restricted, it requires that the others must be flexible should the project need to change. If the time available for development is to be fixed, the quality of what can be achieved must be tailored to fit. Therefore, when planning what an iteration of strictly limited duration can deliver, the only remaining variables are the number and quality of resources, and the quality expectations of the users. Taking this into account, the process to arrive at a plan remains the same as described above, but with the following clarifications:

*   with each iteration limited to a specific number of weeks, its output must be clearly defined. If an iteration cannot produce what was defined or anticipated, a reprioritisation of the Product Backlog may be necessary;
*   the resources required for each iteration are proportionate to the volume of work which must be completed within the agreed time-box;
*   the Sponsor will take particular interest in each iteration, given that it will deliver something which has the potential to release value, or realise benefit.

There are some deliverables and outcomes which are not so easily produced by a process of iteration. For example, the education of customers who are to receive new features or functions may not be best addressed with an incremental solution. The same may be true for the procurement of materials. Therefore, it is often necessary to develop a plan which combines agile and traditionally developed products, as illustrated in the example in Figure 6.12.

This Gantt chart is based on the product flow diagram illustrated in Figure 5.5 and assumes that each iterative cycle is limited to two weeks in duration. Some people-change activity has been added

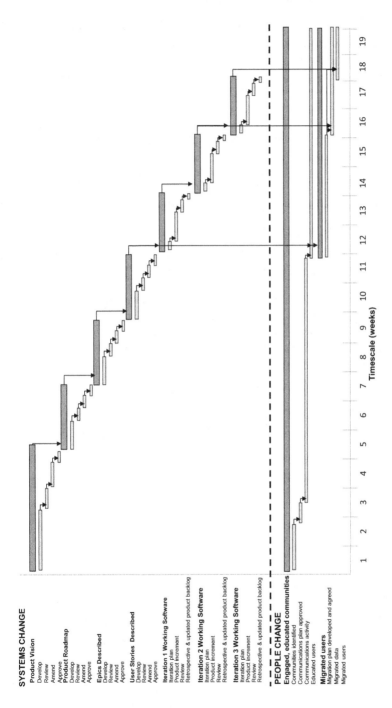

Figure 6.12 Gantt chart agile example.

beneath the dotted line, as has the migration of users to the new system. However, engagement and education have been planned to run continuously alongside the systems development activity. As there is a dependence between the iterative cycles and the migration of users, it has been sensible to accommodate agile and non-agile work within a single plan.

The production and promotion of iteration-specific education and communication materials, and the management of user or customer questions, have been planned to fit within each iterative cycle. Figure 6.13 shows how this has been achieved.

The time-boxed cycle must also include sufficient opportunity to plan what it is to deliver, commencing with the Product Owner's selection of items from the Product Backlog, and taking account of their relative priority and position on the Product Roadmap. In consultation with the Sponsor, consideration must also be given to the value which the iteration promises to release, relative to the cost of its development. Therefore, it is helpful to commence the planning of an iterative cycle with a set of quality criteria by which to judge the fitness for purpose of its eventual output. Following the quality-centric approach described in this chapter, a plan may emerge for the two- or three-week cycle to develop the identified items, review the working output, consider the effectiveness of the team, update the backlog and deploy the product increment.

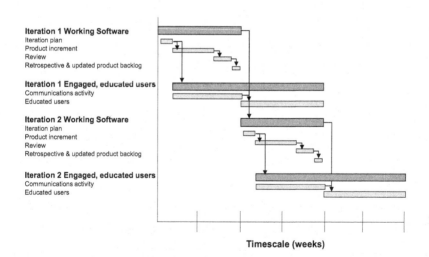

Figure 6.13 Gantt chart hybrid example.

Conclusion

The planning process described in this and the previous chapter has followed a very particular sequence. The creation of a Project Plan is a process that should begin with a reasonable understanding of what the project has to deliver: its products. It should then be possible to determine what resources will be needed and what effort and costs will be expected. Only then will it be possible to produce a timescale. This applies regardless of which development approach is being applied.

At the end of these steps, the plan will contain expressions of how expectations of quality, budget and duration are to be met. They will be consistent because each expression has been built on the back of the other. Even so, it may well be that the plan fails to meet expectations in one or more respects; perhaps the budget is agreeable, but the timescale too long, or the quality may not meet expectation. Consequently, the plan may need to be refined several times before it satisfies as many stakeholders' expectations as possible.

Further reading

Dalkey, Norman; Helmer, Olaf (1963). *An Experimental Application of the Delphi Method to the use of experts. Management Science.* 9 (3): 458–467. doi:10.1287/mnsc.9.3.458.

Herzberg, Frederick. (1993). *Motivation to Work.* London, United Kingdom: Routledge.

ISO 9001:2015. https://www.iso.org/iso-9001-quality-management.html

Murdock, Alexander. (2004). *Personal Effectiveness.* London, United Kingdom: Butterworth-Heinemann Ltd.

Wilson, Randal. (2014). *A Comprehensive Guide to Project Management Schedule and Cost Control: Methods and Models for Managing the Project Lifecycle.* Upper Saddle River, NJ: Pearson FT Press.

7 Identifying and managing risks

Abstract

Much of what might be considered unexpected can be anticipated. Risks are problems which have the potential to damage the project's progress or purpose. From the outset, most projects will promise a certain degree of risk. However, with the right mindset and a supporting process, many risks can be identified, qualified, evaluated and mitigated. Risks, issues, assumptions and dependencies are closely related; management may address them all in a similar way. Chief amongst the mitigations available is contingency. This ensures that there is some time or budget set aside to address risks, issues and changes.

Planning and risk management are continuous; they are as much a mindset as a process.

The principles of risk management

It is helpful to understand the differences between risks, issues and what falls in between. RAID is an acronym which stands for 'risks, assumptions, issues and dependencies'.

- a risk is a challenge to which the project may be exposed, and which may jeopardise it;
- an assumption is a guess – all guesses are risks;
- an issue is a risk that has come to pass and can no longer be prevented or avoided;
- dependencies – the interfaces between deliverables, teams, departments or projects – are areas fraught with risk.

All may be managed using a common set of procedures and mindset. Successful project management seeks to identify and mitigate risks, minimise the likelihood of issues taking place and reduce the number of assumptions made during the life of the project.

An approach to risk management

At any time during the project, but especially when plans are being developed, it is helpful to actively seek areas and instances of risk. Thereafter, a process may be applied to ensure each is suitably addressed (Figure 7.1).

Identify

Some inspiration is helpful when seeking to uncover where the risks may lie in a project. Under the leadership of the Project Manager, the entire project team (including the Project Steering Group) may be encouraged to discover them. Common areas in which risks may be revealed include:

- scope and clarity of requirements;
- politics;
- technology;
- methods;
- resource availability and capability;
- key-person dependencies;
- other areas of dependence;
- any assumptions which have been listed.

The risks may be first captured in a matrix, as illustrated in Figure 7.2.

The advantage of engaging the Project Steering Group in these considerations is not only to benefit from their insight, but to encourage their commitment to the management of the unknown. There are a number of ways in which to mitigate risks; most come at a price. It is therefore sensible that the Sponsor is cognisant of the additional budget – contingency – which may be needed to fund the management and mitigation of risks.

Figure 7.1 Risk management process.

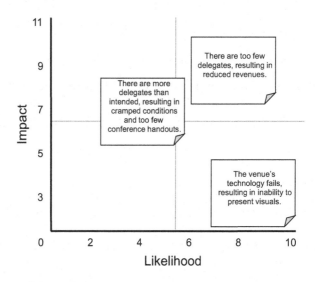

Figure 7.2 Risk matrix.

With debate and discussion, the risks will become more clearly articulated. It is usual to express a risk as a combination of two clauses which, respectively, describe its cause and effect. For example:

• a conference speaker fails to arrive, resulting in disruption to the planned agenda.

The more eloquently the risk is expressed, the easier it becomes to qualify and evaluate.

Qualify

Having articulated each risk, it is then a matter of determining and ranking each in terms of its relative likelihood and impact. This is necessary to determine not only which appears to be most critical but also who may be held ultimately accountable for its mitigation.

'Likelihood' is a measure of the probability that a risk will be realised. Of course, it is not possible to predict that something will be a dead certainty. Thus, the conclusion that a risk is 100% likely identifies it as having already been realised. According to the earlier definitions,

Impact	
0	None – risk has been fully mitigated
3	Activity may be impacted but work can proceed to sign off
5	Product/Stage may be compromised, but no impact on project completion
7	Stage/Project may be compromised, but completion still achievable
9	Project completion may be compromised
11	Organisation/client may suffer
Likelihood	
0	Risk has passed
2	Very low
4	Low
6	Even
8	High
10	Certainty

Figure 7.3 Scale of likelihood and impact.

it is an issue. By the same token, a risk is anything which is considered to be less than certain.

The impact of a risk refers to the effect it may have (or, in the case of an issue, is already having).

It is helpful to ensure that risks and issues are judged consistently. Figure 7.3 provides a measurement scale.

Evaluate

To better understand the relative value of the qualified risks and issues, it is necessary to evaluate the combined effect of their likelihood and impact. This allows for a judgement to be made as to which deserves attention. This is done by creating a risk factor. It is calculated by multiplying together the likelihood and impact. In this way, it may be determined that whilst a prevailing issue has a risk factor of, say, 30, it may be more appropriate to invest precious time or resource into addressing an as-yet unrealised risk which has a higher risk factor of, say, 42.

The risk factor is also helpful in determining who is most suitably authorised to be held accountable for its mitigation, as illustrated in Figure 7.4.

Impact					
11	22	44	66	88	110
9	18	36	54	72	90
7	14	28	42	56	70
5	10	20	30	40	50
3	6	12	18	24	30
0	2	4	6	8	10

Likelihood

SCALE	
0 - 20	Assign to Work stream Leader
21 - 56	Assign to Project Manager
57 - 90	Assign to Project Steering Group
91 - 110	Assign to Portfolio Management Team

Figure 7.4 Risk factor.

Mitigate

This step in the process identifies ways in which the risk may be addressed, preferably in advance of it ever becoming an issue. They include: Accept; Lessen; Avoid; Share. Note that the PRINCE project management methodology identifies five options, including Accept, Reduce, Prevent, Transfer and Contingency. The first four correlate to those listed below. The fifth is described at the end of this chapter.

ACCEPT

The management team accepts that the risk may be realised, but will take no action to mitigate it. In so doing, it is effectively re-categorising the risk as an *assumption.* Although no contingency resources will be set aside and no other action taken, the risk should be monitored in case its likelihood and/or impact should change. For example, it may be accepted that the starting time of a conference may be disrupted by poor weather.

LESSEN

The impact and/or the likelihood of the risk is reduced by the adoption of a mitigating action. For example, the impact of the failure of a projector at a conference may be lessened by having an alternative projector in reserve.

AVOID

The likelihood of a risk is prevented by the adoption of a mitigating action. For example, if a technology solution to a problem is considered too risky, a manual workaround is adopted instead.

SHARE

The burden or cost of mitigation is shared with another party. For example, the cost of the alternative projector noted in the earlier example may be shared with, or transferred to, the venue.

Maintaining a risk-focused approach

The risks are commonly entered into a Risk Register, an example of which is shown in Table 7.1.

The Risk Register becomes the repository for all risks. It may be extended to include a record of assumptions, issues and dependencies. This important management document may be used by the Project Manager to ensure that the mitigating actions are planned, monitored and controlled.

The importance of contingency

Where relevant, a contingency figure has been calculated in the final column, this being an estimate of the time and/or money needed to fund the identified mitigation. For any contingency to be sufficient suggests that it must have been soundly estimated. Everyone involved in the project should be risk-aware, and mindful in their own plans of what contingency they will need.

A contingency fund is also advisable to:

- resolve issues: contingency may be called upon to address problems which were not anticipated;
- facilitate change: contingency provides the funds which may be needed to change or increase the scope of the project;
- assess the impact of change: contingency is the pot from which the funds may be drawn to assess any of the above in order for a solution and proposal to be developed.

It is quite possible that the Sponsor will feel uncomfortable to inflate the budget with contingency that is set aside for something which may not happen. In this case, the amount of contingency may be adjusted

Table 7.1 Risk register

Risk	Likelihood	Impact	Factor	Mitigations	Cost
The venue's technology fails, resulting in inability to present visuals.	8	3	24	Hire backup projector and take to venue on day of conference. Advise venue that they will be invoiced in the event of a projector failure. ACTION: PM	Hire of projector for one day = £/€/$800
There are more delegates than intended, resulting in cramped conditions and too few conference handouts.	4	7	28	1 Reserve a larger room at the venue. ACTION: PM 2 Print a surplus of conference handouts. ACTION: PM	Larger room premium = £/€/$1,000 10% additional handouts = £/€/$500
There are too few delegates, resulting in reduced revenues.	8	9	72	1 Send out additional marketing mailing to previous delegates. ACTION: TL 2 Advise PSG of risk in readiness for possible postponement. ACTION: PM	Marketing mailing = £/€/$400 Postponement losses £/€/$18,500
Total risk-based contingency budget					Maximum £/€/$20,900

according to the likelihood of it being needed. For example, if it is thought that there is a 40% likelihood that there will be insufficient delegates visiting the conference, the contingency budget might be reduced to 40% of the full amount requested by the Project Manager, and adjusted if or when the likelihood changes.

Conclusion

Although much of what has been described in this chapter might be considered as a series of steps through a process, risk management requires the adoption of a particular mindset. Those who profess to be a part of the project's management team can demonstrate their credentials by maintaining a readiness every day to look ahead to the next.

Further reading

Association for Project Management. (2004). *Project Risk Analysis and Management Guide* (2nd ed.). London, United Kingdom: Association for Project Management.

Axelos. (2017). *Managing Successful Projects with PRINCE 2* (6th ed.). London, United Kingdom: Stationery Office.

Hillson, Simon. (2012). *Practical Project Risk Management*. San Francisco, CA: Berrett-Koehler.

Raydugin, Yuri. (2013). *Project Risk Management: Essential Methods for Project Teams and Decision Makers*. Hoboken, NJ: John Wiley & Sons.

Roberts, Paul. (2012). *Strategic Project Management*. London, United Kingdom: Kogan Page Limited.

8 Initiating a project

Abstract

Effective project management begins with effective project initiation. This is the stage during which the management foundations for the project are laid. Fundamental questions about the project are posed and answered before costly resource is committed. As so many people with different perspectives have an interest in the project, it is sensible that the answers to these basic questions are documented. In this way, a clear and common understanding may be shared amongst the project's leaders and managers. The collective and individual expectations of the Project Steering Group are captured in the Business Case. The Project Governance Report (containing the Project Plan) describes how those expectations are to be delivered. As a stage of the project which is consuming resource, it is important that initiation is subject to the same management disciplines outlined for the rest of the project.

Initiation is a time of discovery. It provides an opportunity to confirm whether the Sponsor's vision is viable, whether the plan to deliver it is affordable and realistic and whether there is sufficient enough engagement, agreement and funding for the project to begin.

Although this stage may have a feel of chaos about it, it may be addressed in part with the formality of some key documents which serve as the repositories for the answers to the many questions that will be posed. When initiation is complete, it is crucial that a clear and common understanding and commitment exists amongst the Project Steering Group in order for them to be satisfied that the project can progress.

In Chapter 2, five critical questions were identified which must be answered, understood, documented and agreed by the project's authorities, not merely at the beginning of the project, but throughout its life:

- *Who* needs to be involved in the management of the project?
- *What* must the project deliver?
- *When* must it deliver?
- *How* much must be invested?
- *Why* is this project necessary?

Where an agile development approach has been adopted, the same five questions must be addressed. The project must be commercially justifiable, not only on its own merits, but also when compared to every other endeavour which is competing for scarce resource. The need for leadership and management must be accommodated in a considered organisation structure, taking particular care to include agile-specific roles such as Product Owner and Iteration Leaders. A project plan is just as relevant to this form of development as any other, establishing how time and money are to be spent in pursuit of the features outlined in the Product Backlog. The remaining governance for change control, risk management and communication must also be put in place.

A structured project initiation also helps to provide control, paving a way for the ordered progress as a growing team comes to terms with understanding what, why and how it may meet everyone's expectations of success.

The project initiation

A linear project

The initiation structure illustrated in Figure 8.1 identifies the early key deliverables, approval points and authorities for those projects which are intended to have a traditional, linear lifecycle.

All projects begin with an idea. This is first articulated in the Project Outline. Thereafter, as the idea is transformed through planned activity into deliverables, it may be finally realised as a set of outcomes from which the organisation may benefit. During the initiation stage, the project is formally passed from the Portfolio Management Team to the Project Steering Group. During this time, the project's own, unique and tailored management environment is developed and implemented.

Although it may be called a Project Outline, this articulation of the opportunity or problem being faced by the organisation is not a product of the project itself. The Project Outline is merely a proposal for a project and is commonly produced by anyone in the organisation who is sufficiently enthusiastic to compile and promote it. If such a person

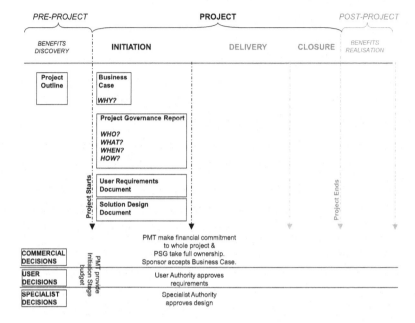

Figure 8.1 Project initiation.

has the commensurate authority and expertise, they may well become the project's eventual Sponsor.

The Project Outline is duly submitted to the Portfolio Management Team who, with knowledge of the entire portfolio of change underway in the organisation, is able to make a decision as to whether or not this particular initiative is to receive some funding. Importantly, once its approval has been granted, the initiative is added to the portfolio pipeline and a limited budget is provided, sufficient enough to fund only its managed initiation. A Sponsor is identified and engaged to direct the initiation stage.

During initiation, the Sponsor must address the question '*Why* is this project necessary?' They will do so through the development of a Business Case. In itself, this may represent a heavy workload, but it is by no means all that must be achieved. The remaining four questions must also be addressed. To do so, it is usual at this time to appoint a Project Manager. Not only can they support the Sponsor in the work required to justify the investment, but they can develop and document the management environment which will be used to govern the project. Thus, the Sponsor and the Project Manager work in concert to, respectively, articulate the vision (captured in the Business Case) and the governance needed to deliver it (described in the Project Governance Report, within which the Project Plan is a major part).

Two further initiation documents may be produced during this period. The first is the User Requirements Document. This articulates the needs of the various communities who will inherit the project's key deliverables. For this very reason, they will be best placed to describe the features which they wish it to possess. The Solution Design Document is produced in response by the specialists who are charged with designing and developing a solution which meets the users' needs. Both are critical expressions which capture vital knowledge and which are fundamental in determining the project's scope. For this reason, although the format and content of such documents will vary from one project to another, both must meet the standards laid down by the User and Specialist Authorities since it is they who must provide their approval when the initiation stage comes to a conclusion.

A project lifecycle accommodating an incremental development approach

In Chapter 2, a comparison was drawn between the lifecycles of projects in which linear and incremental development approaches were being applied. The initiation of the project may be different depending on which development approach – or combination of approaches – is to be used. According to an agile development approach, the requirements or solution do not have to be fully expressed or addressed before the project begins; the product or service is to be developed incrementally and dynamically. Therefore, the dependence on a User Requirements Document and Solution Design Document identified in Figure 8.1 is removed. In their place, the product owner may develop a Product Vision and Product Roadmap to, respectively, outline the intended destination and journey for the product or service. This will lead to the creation of the Product Backlog which lists the prioritised features and functions of the product or service to be delivered. This has the positive consequence that the project may be able to get underway much sooner. It is worth noting that as the project moves into delivery, closure and post-project phases, several of the other deliverables may be different or unnecessary where an agile development approach is being applied. Any such variations are described in later chapters.

Whilst an agile development approach encourages 'working software over comprehensive documentation', there are some project initiation materials which are helpful in describing the management environment within which the project is to be conducted, irrespective of which development approach has been selected. These are described as follows.

Key project initiation materials

Templates for the Business Case and Project Governance Report are available online. Their respective content is as follows.

The Business Case

Opportunity or problem

This section describes why the project is necessary. For example, there may be opportunities to improve the organisation's commercial position by addressing new markets or customers. Conversely, the project may be needed to address a regulatory or mandatory requirement which offers no benefit other than to avoid prosecution.

Strategic fit

The project's profile and lure will be increased if it can be shown how it contributes to the organisation's strategic objectives. In turn, this is more likely to encourage the level of funding being sought.

Interdependencies

If the organisation is used to delivering change in a managed way, the project may form part of a portfolio or programme. It is essential to make clear what relationship exists between it and any other initiatives which are underway or planned. This is not only helpful in managing dependencies and resources. It may also serve the interests of the project to show how benefits may be enabled elsewhere in the organisation were it to be funded.

Success criteria

The results of the work described in Chapter 4 may be included in this section, enabling a clear, full and prioritised set of success criteria to

be expressed. It is only necessary to summarise the commercial measures of success as these will be fully articulated in later sections of the
Business Case.

Options considered

In all likelihood, the Sponsor will have identified a range or variety of
ways in which the opportunity or problem may be addressed. Some
will be more compelling or robust than others. It is important that
they are summarised for comparison and contrast. In this way, an unpalatable selected option may appear all the more attractive for being
the best of a range of poor alternatives. Specifically, it is always helpful
to describe the 'do nothing' option. Oddly, this may help to justify the
project. For example, a compelling case may be made for a project to
comply with a regulatory change if it can be shown that to do nothing
would require the organisation to pay a fine.

Selected option

The option identified here is whichever appears, on the basis of analysis included in the Business Case, to be the most commercially, practically, technically and politically attractive.

SELECTED OPTION: RISKS

In order to present a balanced argument, the Business Case must be
more than a promotional document. In identifying and describing a
summary of the project's risks, the Sponsor is able to inject further
realism, and ensure that, if funding is provided, an additional contingency fund may be justified. This section will be a development of the
risks identified in the Project Outline

SELECTED OPTION: BENEFITS

Every benefit is to be described, showing how each is to be measured
and commercially quantified. As described in Chapter 4, their value
should be shown over time.

SELECTED OPTION: COSTS

Just as every benefit is identified and quantified, so too should every
cost. These should not be only those expected during the life of the

project. Post-project operational, maintenance and support costs must also be included. This is because the benefits of a project are unlikely to be realised until well after it has been closed. Running costs will also accrue over that same period.

SELECTED OPTION: COST/BENEFIT ANALYSIS

When the costs and benefits are shown together across the same time period, a realistic comparison may be drawn. For funding purposes, this becomes the commercial heart of the Business Case. Furthermore, the quantification techniques described in Chapter 4 may be reliably applied to provide a realistic expectation of how the organisation's investment may perform. The format should be as shown in Tables 4.3 and 4.4 in Chapter 4.

SELECTED OPTION: DELIVERABLES AND TIMESCALES

This section summarises what the project will deliver and by when. Only target dates for key milestones need be included. However, some high-level Product Descriptions may provide additional insight and inspire confidence.

SELECTED OPTION: PLANNING ASSUMPTIONS

Planning is educated guesswork, and those considering the Business Case will wish to know how the numbers and dates quoted were arrived at. A list of planning assumptions must be included which fully describe the calculations in the Business Case.

SELECTED OPTION: BENEFITS REALISATION PLAN

As the period of benefits realisation may take some time, the Sponsor should describe how each benefit is to be measured, tracked and delivered.

The project governance report

Working in partnership with the Sponsor as they develop the Business Case, the Project Manager must produce the Project Governance Report in response, showing how the time and money being requested will be used to deliver products of sufficient enough quality to allow for the eventual realisation of the proposed benefits. Note that in the PRINCE project management methodology, the Business Case and

Project Governance Report are combined into what is called a Project Initiation Document.

As the Sponsor sought to answer the question, *Why is this project necessary?* the Project Manager must address the four which remain:

- *Who* needs to be involved in the management of the project?
- *What* must the project deliver?
- *When* must it deliver?
- *How* much must be invested?

The Project Governance Report is merely the repository for the answers to these vital questions. Nevertheless, it serves to show both what is known and unknown about the project. In this way, it demonstrates how ready the project appears for a confident transition into the delivery stage, the decision for which is put to the Project Steering Group.

Commonly, the following sections are to be found in a Project Governance Report:

Organisation

ORGANISATION: ORGANISATION CHART

The project's organisation structure may be best represented in the form shown in Figure 3.2 with the names of the selected incumbents identified in the relevant boxes.

ORGANISATION: ROLES AND RESPONSIBILITIES

As every project is different, so too may be the responsibilities associated with each role. It is helpful to start with a set of clear and commonly understood role descriptions (such as those which are available online). These may then be tailored according to the particular nature of the project, and to the specific character of the incumbents themselves. In this way, the role descriptions may be used to ensure that everyone is clear about what their role entails.

ORGANISATION: COMMUNICATIONS PLAN

A communications plan is needed to show how the project's stakeholders are to be engaged. It must describe:

- what information is to be communicated within the project, to the wider organisation and, possibly, the outside world;

- the audiences who are to be engaged;
- what form the communication should take;
- when it will be needed.

Any such plan should allow for the fact that communications are two-way. When considering the format, it is sensible to plan how the identified audiences may also actively engage with the project.

In addressing these points, the communications plan may take the following form:

- a table which lists the various audiences and their respective information needs;
- an associated list of the methods of communications which will be used, together with dates and frequencies.

Project plan

This dynamic document shows how the Project Steering Group's vision, described in the Business Case, can be delivered by the project team within known constraints which include, but are not limited to, time and budget.

This version of the plan shows the project as it is known and understood at the point of initiation. It is used by the Project Steering Group to confirm that each participant understands how the various resources are to be used to deliver their respective parts of the vision. It is also retained to be used as a measure against which progress – and any future variances – may be compared. In this way, it will be possible to determine the extent to which the project is on track. This original version of the plan is referred to as a *baseline*. With this purpose in mind, once approved, it should not be amended in any way in order to serve its purpose as a record of the project at the point of its initiation.

Since planning is an iterative process, the plan may also be used by the Project Manager to determine whether the vision is achievable within the various constraints set down by the Project Steering Group. Several cycles of planning may be required to arrive at a compromise which marries the ambition of the vision with the available resources.

Commonly, a Project Plan will be composed of four key parts:

- a quality plan;
- a resource plan;
- a time schedule;
- project controls.

PROJECT PLAN: QUALITY PLAN

In this section, the Project Manager may describe how the project will meet the standards expected of the project's end product. The greater the expectation of quality, the higher the likely cost and the longer the probable duration of the project. Therefore, it follows that the individual plans for quality, time and cost must be aligned for the whole to be considered robust and achievable.

PROJECT PLAN: QUALITY PLAN DELIVERABLES

In this section, the Project Manager may describe not merely the project's specified end product, but also all of the other deliverables which lead to it. This forms one expression of the scope of the project. A Product Breakdown Structure, as described in Chapter 5, may serve as an illustration.

Since it is important to remove any chance of misunderstanding, each deliverable may be described more fully by means of a Product Description. In a larger or more complex project, these may be tabulated so that they are more easily scrutinised and comprehended by members of the Project Steering Group. However, the deliverables are described, it is vital that they are brought to the attention of these senior people. This is their only exposure to any form of expression that describes what they will get for their investment.

It may also be helpful to show the products in their sequence of delivery, so that dependencies within the project, and interdependencies with areas outside of it, may be properly understood. A Product Flow Diagram, described in Chapter 5, can serve this purpose.

PROJECT PLAN: QUALITY PLAN RESPONSIBILITIES

The purpose of the plan is to show how the project's objectives may be achieved. As one such objective is to deliver products of a specified standard, it follows that it must also be made clear who is responsible and accountable for which management aspects of quality, including:

- its specification;
- its planning;
- its build;
- its testing;
- its acceptance.

PROJECT PLAN: QUALITY PLAN STANDARDS

Here, the Project Manager is able to list any prescribed standards, procedures or methods which may contribute to the end product's fitness for purpose. There may be documentary or procedural standards relevant to:

- specifying the requirements;
- designing the solution;
- building the solution;
- testing the solution;
- operating the end product;
- managing the project.

PROJECT PLAN: PLANNING ASSUMPTIONS

The Project Manager may include an Estimating Sheet, described in Chapter 6 and illustrated in Table 6.1.

PROJECT PLAN: TIME SCHEDULE

A Gantt chart, like the one illustrated in Figure 6.6, may be used to show how the project's products will be scheduled for delivery over the duration of the project. Alternatively, a Product Flow Diagram, as illustrated in Figure 5.2, embellished with planned delivery dates may serve the same purpose, and be a more palatable read for the Project Steering Group.

PROJECT PLAN: RESOURCE PLAN

A resource plan, as illustrated in Table 6.2, allows the Project Steering Group to understand what resources will be required for the project, when they are needed and at what individual and total cost.

PROJECT PLAN: RISKS

Here, the Project Manager can include a further refinement of the risk analysis which began in the Project Outline and was developed in the Business Case. As the Project Plan must describe how the project is to be managed, it follows that each risk must be accompanied and addressed by one or more mitigations. This will demonstrate to the Project Steering Group that not only have the risks been identified, but that there is also a plan to manage the project's exposure to these threats.

The risk register, described in Table 7.1, provides a way of presenting the risk management plan, and has the added advantage of identifying an appropriate and considered contingency budget.

PROJECT PLAN: PROJECT CONTROLS

Without control, a plan is merely an aspiration. Therefore, this section allows the Project Manager to describe what management tools and techniques will be used to keep the project on track once it has received the Project Steering Group's approval to commence.

PROJECT PLAN: PROJECT CONTROLS (MEETINGS AND REPORTING)

This section is where the Project Manager describes which methods will be used to monitor and report the project's progress, and to control its further passage. It may include:

- the project initiation meeting: the event at which the Project Steering Group meet to consider, challenge and approve or decline the Project Governance Report;
- team progress meetings: regular events which allow the Project Manager to delegate work and to take feedback from the team as to its progress;
- other Project Steering Group meetings: meetings which are aligned to key delivery or decision-making points in the project at which engagement is needed from the Project Steering Group;
- the project closure meeting: one of the last occasions on which the Project Steering Group will meet, at which a decision may or may not be taken to close the project;
- the Lessons Learned Review: an event which allows for the management of the project to be considered with the benefit of hindsight such that improvements may be recommended for adoption;
- the Benefits Realisation Review(s): events after the project has closed which allow the Sponsor to assess the extent to which the intended benefits were realised, and at what eventual cost.

PROJECT PLAN: PROJECT CONTROLS (ESCALATION MANAGEMENT)

This section is used to describe and agree the conditions under which control may pass from the Project Manager to the Project Steering Group in the event that the project is no longer forecast to complete as planned. This subject is described further in Chapter 9.

The Project Governance Report describes the scale of forecast variance needed to escalate control from the Project Manager to the Project Steering Group, and what process must be followed if the escalation conditions are met. Typically, it may be agreed that the Project Manager will immediately alert the Project Steering Group, offering it a proposal which allows the participants to understand the nature of the forecast variance, the options to address it, the impact which each would have on the plan and Business Case and the Project Manager's recommended option.

PROJECT PLAN: PROJECT CONTROLS (CHANGE CONTROL)

This section describes how changes will be managed, if and when they occur. To facilitate effective change management, it is necessary to know which of the key project artefacts may be impacted and, therefore, which need to be used as a baseline against which to determine the scale and impact of the change. Commonly, these will include:

*   the Business Case: to understand the impact on the forecast benefits;
*   the Project Governance Report: to understand the impact which the change may have on project timescales, costs and risks;
*   the User Requirements Document (and/or the Product Backlog): to understand the impact on the scope and quality of the project;
*   the Solution Design Document: to determine the impact on the proposed solution.

Contingency amounts and sources can be identified, and a process described by which all agree to abide if something occurs which requires, or may result in, a change to one or more of the above.

This subject is described further in Chapter 9.

PROJECT PLAN: PROJECT CONTROLS (CONFIGURATION CONTROL)

This section describes how control will be maintained of the products created by the project. It may be helpful to describe how their version control, ownership and accountability, storage and security are to be managed

PROJECT PLAN: PROJECT CONTROLS (QUALITY CONTROL)

This section describes the methods that will be used to review and test key products to ensure they meet the desired standard.

PROJECT PLAN: PROJECT CONTROLS (RISK AND ISSUE MANAGEMENT)

This section describes how risks and issues will be identified and managed, including the way in which the Project Manager may draw on contingency funds if/when necessary.

Conclusion

The initiation stage is an opportunity to replace chaos with sufficient enough order that the project is given the greatest chances of success. It can produce:

- a well-balanced Project Steering Group;
- an identified and recruited Project Manager;
- a Business Case which forecasts an acceptable margin between costs and benefits;
- customer requirements that are clearly and fully articulated – or an agreement to develop them incrementally according to a product vision and roadmap;
- a Solution Design Document which addresses them;
- a means of describing (in the Project Governance Report, especially the Project Plan) how the project will meet the targets set out in the Business Case;
- a clear and common understanding of the answers to all five key questions:
  - Who needs to be involved in the management of the project?
  - What must the project deliver?
  - When must it deliver?
  - How much must be invested?
  - Why is this project necessary?

The work undertaken during the initiation stage to address these questions provides the foundation on which the project's progress can be monitored and controlled.

Further reading

Axelos. (2017). *Managing Successful Projects with PRINCE 2* (6th ed.). London, United Kingdom: Stationery Office.
Roberts, Paul. (2020). *Guide to Change and Project Management* (3rd ed.). London, United Kingdom: Profile Books.

9 Keeping a project under control

Abstract

With an approved plan in place, it becomes vital to control progress. This begins by ensuring that the work has been suitably packaged and delegated. Thereafter, the team's progress is monitored to determine if there has been any divergence from the plan. The Project Manager can use a Project Forecast Report to do so at a product/deliverable level. The Project Steering Group will be concerned to know that the benefits and other measures of success forecast in the Business Case may still be realised. Each member of the project's management team has a range of corrective options at their disposal to ensure that progress is maintained. The quality of the project's deliverables can be scrutinised prior to formal approval, ensuring that the project leaves behind it a complement of products that facilitate the realisation of benefits. Crucially, accepting that the project exists in a changing environment, the governance allows for changes, whether planned or not, to be sufficiently assessed before any decision to address them is made. Where an agile approach to development has been chosen, many of these controls can be alternatively or additionally undertaken within each iteration.

The following diagram identifies the stages in a cycle of progress management (Figure 9.1).

Accepting that the project will be subject to challenges and changes, this continuous cycle contains a series of steps which determine if a corrective intervention is needed to keep the project on track. How often a manager exercises control in this way depends on

- their personal aversion to risk;
- the direction of those in the management structure above them;
- the urgency and importance of the work;

Figure 9.1 Control cycle.

- the volume of work to be undertaken;
- the present position in the project lifecycle;
- the expertise of the people doing the work;
- the approach being used to develop the product or service (e.g. agile).

All of the activities in the cycle are important, but none count for much if corrective action – control – is not taken in sufficient time to prevent planned progress from failing. It is for this reason that it is called a *control* cycle.

As indicated in the final bullet above, the way in which control is exercised depends in part on which development approach – or combinations of approach – is being employed within the project. The following sections describe the common controls applied in a linear development lifecycle. Those which may be used in an agile development approach are described at the end of this chapter.

Management by exception

In Chapter 3, several levels of authority were identified which influence the project:

- Portfolio Management Team;
- Project Steering Group;
- Project Manager;
- Workstream Leaders.

Not only must the control cycle be used effectively by each of these managers, there must also be a means of escalating matters upwards when one of them has insufficient authority to rule on a certain matter or make a decision. This is called 'management by exception'. It ensures that when the control cycle has identified the need for corrective action, it is executed by that person or people with the appropriate level of authority.

In the context of the Project Manager's relationship with their Project Steering Group, it is important to understand what is to be done if the project is no longer forecast to complete as planned. As described in the Project Governance Report, there must be clarity about who has the authority to manage the project when issues arise or changes become necessary. Under normal conditions – where progress is taking place according to the plan – the Project Manager has the Project Steering Group's authority to manage the project on its behalf. However, circumstances may arise where the Project Manager realises that the project is no longer forecast to complete as planned. The Project Steering Group may have assumed that its Project Manager has the authority needed to bring the project back on track. In point of fact, the *scale* of the forecast variance from plan is of enormous importance. If the variance is within pre-defined limits, it is true that the Project Manager has the authority to take the corrective action necessary to bring the project back on track. However, the Project Steering Group needs to be informed if the forecast variance is of such significance that its intervention and greater authority are needed to address the cause. Therefore, it is important for the Project Steering Group to have set and agreed some escalation conditions with its Project Manager at the initiation of the project.

In this way, if or when the project is no longer forecast to complete as planned, the extent of the variance may be measured. If the variance breaches the Project Manager's pre-defined limits, the matter is escalated automatically to the Project Steering Group. As the highest authority in the project, it has the power to decide what action must be taken to bring the project back on track, or to authorise the development of a revised plan.

For example, if the escalation conditions for time and cost have been set for ± one week and ± 7% respectively, the Project Steering Group need not be involved in the daily management of the project as long as its *forecast* end date does not vary by more or less than a week and the *forecast* cost remains within ±7% of its target. If the Project Manager's forecast suggests that the variance will be greater, control is temporarily passed to the Project Steering Group until a solution has been identified, planned and approved.

Often, red, amber and green (RAG) reporting is used to facilitate this approach, where:

- red denotes a breach of time and/or budget escalation conditions;
- amber identifies that the project is not forecast to deliver on time and/or budget, but that the authority to bring it back on track remains within the Project Manager;
- green indicates that the project remains on target for time and budget.

This scale and manner of reporting facilitates effective project control.

The control cycle: plan

As previous chapters have demonstrated, the plan is what describes how time and budget will be used to produce deliverables that meet the standard required of them.

The control cycle: delegate

Work is delegated from one person to another. The ideal is to provide sufficient information for the work to be undertaken with the need for as little supervision as possible. Delegation typically occurs between one level of authority and another, for example the Project Steering Group delegates responsibility for the development of the Project Governance Report to the Project Manager. Similarly, the Project Manager may delegate responsibility for the development of other key deliverables to members of the project team or to Workstream Leaders.

When delegating, it is important to make clear what is needed, and under what conditions or constraints the work must be undertaken. Effective delegation depends on the clarity of understanding imparted by the 'delegator' to the 'delegatee'. This will include some knowledge about the work to be done – especially the product which is to be created – and the extent of the delegatee's authority to operate without recourse to the delegator.

Thus, when work is to be delegated within, or from within, a project, it is important for both parties to seek clarity and agreement about:

- what is expected from the delegatee (a Product Description can be used to make this clear);
- when the work is due to begin and end (an extract from the Time Schedule can show this);

- how much budget (money or person-days effort) is available to de-velop the product (an extract from the Resource Plan can show this);
- who and what else is dependent on the product(s) to be delivered, and which products they will require (a Product Flow Diagram can help to illustrate this);
- which previously developed products may be needed to develop the new product.

This advances an understanding of what is expected from the delega-tee. However, whilst they have responsibility to produce what has been agreed, the delegator remains accountable for the outcome. Therefore, it can be helpful for both parties to also agree:

- how the delegatee will charge their time or cost to the appropriate project account so the delegator can monitor spending;
- what skills and experience will be required of the delegatee;
- who will be held accountable for the successful completion of the work;
- when and how the delegator and delegatee will monitor and report progress;
- what escalation terms are to be used in the event of any risk to the timescale or budget being identified, thereby enabling the delega-tor to intervene well in advance of the targets being breached;
- what specific techniques, processes or procedures should be adopted by the delegatee.

Such terms often form the basis of a formal arrangement between two parties, particularly where work is delegated to an external supplier or partner. This may become the basis for a contract or a 'terms of reference'.

The control cycle: monitor, report and control

Understanding the actual state of the project, writing down those ob-servations and taking the corrective action necessary to address any untoward variances should form a seamless sequence. Some monitor-ing, reporting and control mechanisms are administered by the Pro-ject Steering Group, and some by the Project Manager.

Monitoring, reporting and control mechanisms used by the Project Steering Group

A Project Steering Group will benefit from a control cycle that regu-larly informs it of the project's status. It must also be confident that it will be alerted by the Project Manager if the project appears no longer able to meet its planned completion targets.

A Project Steering Group can use the following as a means of control:

- project initiation and closure;
- stage meetings;
- unscheduled Project Steering Group meetings;
- scheduled Project Steering Group meetings;
- project forecast reporting.

Project initiation and closure

See Chapters 8 and 10.

Scheduled stage meetings

Scheduled stage meetings provide an opportunity for the Project Steering Group to assess the present and forecast state of the Business Case. This serves to ascertain whether the project remains on track to deliver an outcome where the benefits still promise to outweigh the costs by an agreeable margin. The opportunity may also be used for the Project Manager to demonstrate to the Project Steering Group that the performance of the project during the previous stage was as planned, and to offer a plan for the next stage for the Project Steering Group to approve before any further money or resource is committed to the project. In this way, a stage meeting represents a moment in the project's lifecycle when it is temporarily halted in order that the Project Steering Group can consciously and intentionally decide whether or not it can and should continue.

If, as is often the case, Project Steering Group meetings take place regularly (and not merely when there is a project stage break), it is common for the Project Manager to circulate and present a Project Forecast Report. As described later in this chapter, this provides a snapshot in time of the project's status, and a forecast of its ability to meet its time, cost and quality targets.

Unscheduled project steering group meeting

An unscheduled meeting of the Project Steering Group may be convened if, as described earlier, the Project Manager reports that the project is no longer forecast to complete as planned by a margin which breaches the agreed escalation conditions. In this way, the Project

Steering Group can safely assume that, until or unless the Project Manager tells them otherwise, 'no news is good news'.

Monitoring, reporting and control mechanisms used by the Project Manager

The Project Manager's principal responsibility is to motivate and manage the team to produce the specified deliverables on time, on budget and to the agreed standard. Any of these expectations may be impacted by changes that have been requested, or problems that may have arisen. As described earlier, time, cost and quality are interdependent; a change to one will probably have an impact on another. It follows that if the Project Manager is to maintain control, they will benefit from some management information which informs them when and where to intervene. The following monitoring and reporting mechanisms are the absolute essentials to facilitate effective control.

Project team progress meeting

The control cycle described earlier may be put into practice as a means for the Project Manager to manage the project team's work. Over the course of, say, two weeks, the Project Manager must plan what must be delivered, delegate work, monitor progress against the plan, report and communicate to the project's stakeholders (especially the Project Steering Group) and take corrective action if or where there have been variances. Figure 9.2 illustrates the control cycle as a series of project management events spread over a fortnight and centred on a meeting of the project team.

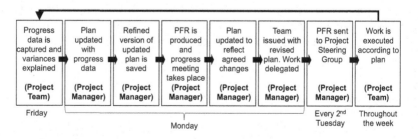

Figure 9.2 Project control events.

The Project Forecast Report is a repository of reliable and trustworthy management information which may be used to identify where the project will benefit from corrective action.

Project forecast reports

These are sometimes called Project Status Reports or Project Progress Reports. However, both titles imply that they are describing the position of the project *at present*. Managers need to know whether the project's completion criteria may still be met. Value comes from a report which *predicts* the state of the project at the point at which it is expected to complete. In this way, it forecasts the extent to which the budget will have been used up, whether the end date will have been met and what deliverables will have been produced.

By presenting carefully selected information, the Project Forecast Report allows the Project Manager to communicate with the team, the Project Steering Group and (if necessary) the Portfolio Management Team.

There is a wealth of management information which may be included in such a report. The following illustration contains only that which is considered absolutely essential to facilitate effective management by the Project Manager, the Project Steering Group and/or the Portfolio Management Team.

The Project Manager needs enough detailed information to monitor the progress of individuals in the team. This detail is the source from which the summary has been drawn in order to identify specific instances of variance and the reasons for it. The source from which nearly all of this information comes is the Project Plan. It follows that, for the whole reporting hierarchy to be sustainable, the core data in the Project Plan must be up-to-date and accurate.

A detailed Project Forecast Report can be substantial, especially for large or complex projects. Since the Project Manager must control timescales, costs, quality and risks, it is usual for the Project Forecast Report to reflect that content at a level of detail commensurate with the plan and the need to control.

Terms used in the Project Forecast Report are described as follows:

• Baseline: This is what was originally agreed by the Project Steering Group and is used as a yardstick against which progress – and variances from plan – may be measured. Many things may be baselined, including the benefits, the budget and the project's end date. These will be as documented in the versions of the Business

Case and Project Governance Report that were approved during the Initiation Stage. Given the importance of having a reliable measure against which comparisons may be made, it follows that any baseline should remain unchanged, unless the Project Steering Group provides their authority to do so. These circumstances will be described further when considering how changes are managed.

- Actual to date (ATD): These are measures which should increase over time. For example, Resource 1 may have committed £/€/$7,000 of a baseline £/€/$10,000 budget. Thus, the ATD is £/€/$7,000.
- Estimate to complete (ETC): Arguably, this is one of the most important items of management information. It is the most recent estimate, representing the most up-to-date information available regarding the amount outstanding. It is not merely a subtraction of the ATD from the baseline since this would assume that the original estimate remained correct, which it may not be. For example, if the ATD is £/€/$7,000 and the baseline was £/€/$10,000, it does not follow that the ETC is £/€/$3,000. Since approving the baseline, costs may have increased. Therefore, the Project Forecast Report must reflect this. If the ETC is £/€/$5,000, the new total is £/€/$12,000 (ATD + ETC), known as the forecast at completion.
- Forecast at completion (FAC): This is the sum of ATD and ETC (£/€/$12,000 in the example described earlier).
- Variance: This is the difference between the baseline and the FAC. To continue the example, it is minus £/€/$2,000 (the baseline £/€/$10,000 less the forecast at completion £/€/$12,000). This figure may be compared with the escalation criteria to calculate the extent of the variance, and thereby determine if the matter must be escalated.

The sections contained in the Project Forecast Report mirror the general content and structure of the Project Plan.

TIME FORECAST

Products and milestones from the plan are shown in the time forecast section, illustrated in Figure 9.3. Not all need be shown, only those which are considered deserving of management attention, perhaps because they are on the critical path, are risky or are of special importance to the Project Steering Group. In this example, only end dates have been shown. However, it can be helpful to include start dates too, since knowing if something has begun on time can be an indication of whether it will finish according to plan.

Time Forecast	Baseline	Actual or forecast End Date	Variance	Reason	Condition (Red/ Amber/ Green)	Action/ Responsibility
Deliverable 4	10/08	15/08	-5		Red	
Deliverable 7	14/10	15/10	-1		Amber	
Project Closure	11/11	11/11	0		Green	

Budget Forecast	Baseline A	Actual To Date B	Estimate To Complete C	Forecast At Completion D (B+C)	Variance E (D-A)	Reason	Condition (Red/ Amber/ Green)	Action/ Responsibility
Resource 1 (£/€/$)	10,000	7,000	5,000	12,000	-2,000		Amber	
Resource 2 (£/€/$)	13,000	3,000	8,000	11,000	2,000		Amber	
TOTAL (£/€/$)	23,000	10,000	13,000	23,000	0		Green	

Quality Forecast	Baseline A	Actual To Date B	Estimate To Complete C	Forecast At Completion D (B+C)	Variance E (D-A)	Reason	Condition (Red/ Amber/ Green)	Action/ Responsibility
e.g. Migrated records	1,500	40	900	940	-560		Red	

Risk Management	ID	Risk	Likelihood A	Impact B	Factor C (AxB)	Mitigation	Condition (Red/ Amber/ Green)	Action/ Responsibility
Risks requiring PSG action	3	There are too few delegates, resulting in reduced revenues.	8	9	72	PSG approve use of contingency fund for additional mailings	Amber	

Figure 9.3 Project forecast report.

BUDGET FORECAST

There are a number of ways of reporting the costs of the project. Figure 9.3 lists the costs by resource type, and can include people and non-human costs. An alternative is to list the costs by product. A further variation is to separate the capital, revenue and human revenue costs, showing them as three summarised rows. Note that when the numbers are homogenised in a summary, it may be difficult to determine the source of any identified variance.

QUALITY FORECAST

In addition to being presented with time and budgetary information, the Project Steering Group will want reassurance that the project is likely to meet its quality targets. The example shown in Figure 9.3 identifies a specific measure of success and shows how close the project is to meeting it. Here, it suggests that the number of records being migrated from one system to another will fall short of the intended target. This may call into question whether the project's resources are being used effectively, or if the solution will be delivered to the intended standard. In either case, the project's management team deserves to know so that corrective action may be taken where needed.

The risks and issues recorded in the Project Forecast Report are those which deserve to be identified for the attention of the Project Steering Group, as denoted by the value of the risk factor. A scale suggesting to whom a risk or issue must be escalated for attention is shown in Chapter 7, Figure 7.4.

Project benefit forecast

The Sponsor may wish the Project Manager to help maintain the Business Case in between stages. In addition to the summary shown in Figure 9.3, it may be desirable for a periodic review of the forecast costs and benefits. Commonly, the incurred costs may be taken into account when revisiting the cost/benefit analysis in the Business Case. However, it may also be possible or necessary to refine the estimated benefits. This may be because the original estimates are thought to be wrong or out-of-date, or because some of the benefits have already been delivered. An example is shown in Figure 9.4.

Earned value analysis

Earned value analysis objectively measures the project's accomplishments in respect of its performance against time, cost and quality targets. It depends on a fully articulated and maintained plan being available and relies on being able to calculate the extent to which any product is complete. Therefore, it is a prerequisite that the plan against which progress is being tracked is product-based.

Benefit Forecast	Baseline A	Actual To Date B	Estimate To Complete C	Forecast At Completion D (B+C)	Variance E (D-A)	Reason	Condition (Red/ Amber/ Green)	Action/ Responsibility
Increased employee satisfaction resulting in reduced costs associated with staff wastage (£/ €/$)	30,000	5,000	25,000	30,000	0		Green	
Removal of redundant IT hardware resulting in reduced licence costs (£/ €/$)	85,000	15,000	70,000	85,000	0		Green	
TOTAL (£/ €/$)	115,000	20,000	95,000	115,000	0		Green	

Figure 9.4 Project benefit forecast report.

For example, it may be known from progress reporting that the actual costs have exceeded the planned costs. This may be considered a positive development. However, it takes no account of what has actually been delivered. If the project were to finish suddenly in spite of being under budget, it may also have failed to produce everything that was expected.

Assuming that a product-based plan is in place, it should be possible to determine the value of each product and its total cost of production. Shown over time, this is called the planned value. At the end of every period, it is possible to calculate the value of every product created so far, allowing a proportionate amount for partially completed products. This is the earned value. As progress is tracked, instead of simply comparing the planned and actual cost, it is instead possible to compare the earned value of delivered products with their expected planned value.

An earned value which is higher than the actual cost implies that the products delivered thus far have contributed a greater value than the spend to date. Conversely, a lower earned value may indicate a failure to meet the standard expected, or an over-spend which has outweighed the value of the product.

The following are terms commonly used to facilitate the use of earned value analysis:

- budgeted cost of work scheduled (BCWS): the budgeted cost of work planned in the period being measured;
- budgeted cost of work performed (BCWP): the planned cost of work completed in the period being measured.
- actual cost of work performed (ACWP): the cost of work actually completed to date.

With such measures, it is possible to calculate:

- cost variation: the budgeted cost of work scheduled minus the actual cost of work planned (how much should have been spent to date based on what has been achieved, minus the amount which has actually been spent);
- schedule variation: the budgeted cost of work performed minus the budgeted cost of work scheduled (how much should have been spent to date based on what has been achieved, minus the amount that was planned to have been spent);
- schedule delay: when the budgeted cost of work scheduled is the same as the budgeted cost of work performed, less the date when the data was captured, measured in days.

Quality reviews

As described in Chapter 5, a project's success depends very much on being able to describe and deliver products which meet a particular standard. The quality criteria form a major part of the product's description and can be employed as a checklist against which the developed product may be measured. A quality review is a form of test which determines the extent to which a product meets the desired standard and may be considered 'finished'.

A quality review is a managed process for comparing the developed draft product to the Product Description, allowing for corrections to be adopted and approval provided.

Different forms of quality review are suited to different types of product:

- test: involving a physical examination;
- inspection: where a product or service is subjected to visual scrutiny;
- demonstration: where possible faults are identified by a walk-through or presentation;
- formal quality review: where a body of reviewers measures the extent to which the draft product meets the standard expected of it as defined in the Product Description;
- informal quality review: a less exacting version of a formal quality review, allowing for the use of email or social applications to facilitate the identification and correction of errors.

Figure 9.5 illustrates the lifecycle of a product, being the context within which it is tested.

Change control

It is quite normal for things to change during the life of a project. Some changes may be relatively trivial, perhaps identified by scrutiny of a Project Forecast Report, or through a conversation with a member of the team. The Project Manager has the authority to manage such variances as long as they do not result in the project being forecast to miss its agreed targets by more than the escalation conditions allow. As described earlier, if a breach of those conditions was to be forecast, the Project Manager would be duty-bound to escalate the matter to the Project Steering Group.

However, sometimes a change is considered necessary, not because something has 'gone wrong', but because it is *desirable*. Therefore,

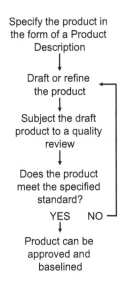

Figure 9.5 Quality review process.

whilst Project Managers are responsible for steering the project within escalation tolerances, they must also manage *requests for change;* applications which propose that an aspect of the project is altered in some way. This may include increasing or decreasing its scope, amending its delivery date or budget or something more substantial such as merging it with another project.

The request for change may seem very reasonable to the person who makes it. However, Project Managers must be careful to avoid being persuaded to change the plan simply by the power of an argument, especially if it comes from a senior member of the management or leadership team. Rather, they must ensure that the *consequences* of a proposed change are fully understood so that its possible impact on the project's target delivery date, budget, quality, risk profile and benefits are known. Only in this way can a considered, informed and auditable decision be made as to the relative merits of the change request.

As a result, it is quite possible that the project, on having accommodated a request for change, may appear very different as a result. Its timescale may be extended, its budget doubled or its products delivered to a markedly different standard from that originally planned. However, as long as these changes are agreed under predetermined management conditions and that overall the project remains commercially

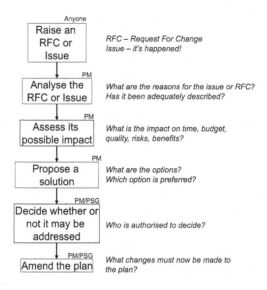

Figure 9.6 Change control process.

justifiable, they may be considered a very normal feature in the life of a project.

Figure 9.6 illustrates a process which accommodates the points raised earlier.

- Request for change or issue? Anyone inside or outside the project may raise an issue or propose a change.
- Change request analysis. It is usual to complete a form which fully describes the reason for the change, or the nature of the issue. Supporting material may be needed.
- Impact assessment. The issue or change request is assessed to determine the extent of the variation which it may cause. The consequences on both the Project Plan and the Business Case must be quantified.
- Solution proposal. A solution to the issue or request for change is identified. Several options may be explored, but there must be a clear recommendation.
- Decision. Who takes the decision is dependent on knowing the extent to which the recommended course of action creates a forecast deviation from the baseline. If the change request is considered suitable for inclusion and can be accommodated within the

Project Manager's agreed escalation conditions, the decision is theirs. If the change request is considered to be worthy of inclusion but renders the project unable to complete within the Project Manager's forecast escalation conditions, only the Project Steering Group has the authority to decide.

• Amend plan. The Project Manager updates the plan to reflect the outcome, including the creation of a set of revised baselines against which future progress will be measured, as necessary.

Dependent on scale, the Project Manager or Project Steering Group may provide funds from the contingency budget to pay for the management of this process, and also for the work required during analysis, assessment and solution proposal. Furthermore, the contingency fund may well be needed to pay for the implementation of the change (or to solve an issue), if authorised.

Corrective action

Any corrective action identified by a project management team will have a consequence on one or more of the project's baselined features, be it time, cost, quality, risk or benefits. For example, if more time is needed, the costs of the project are likely to rise. Alternatively, if the budget is found to be insufficient, quality may be impacted. The Project Steering Group may consider some of these features to be more important – or less flexible – than others. This reduces the range and effectiveness of the corrective actions available to the Project Manager, as follows:

To accommodate a change without…:

• changing the project's end date, the Project Manager may…:
  • increase resourcing;
  • increase productivity;
  • reduce quality expectations;
  • reduce the project's scope.
• increasing the project's budget, the Project Manager may…:
  • engage cheaper resources;
  • engage fewer resources;
  • reduce quality expectations;
  • reduce the project's scope;
  • amend project delivery dates;
  • increase productivity.

- reducing the original expectations for quality and content, the Project Manager may...:
  - increase resourcing;
  - increase productivity;
  - improve quality processes, including tests;
  - challenge or revise customer expectations;
  - delay project delivery dates;
  - offer discounts;
  - defer some delivery until later in – or after – the project.

Whilst unpalatable, a change may require the project:

- to be later than originally planned;
- to spend more than originally planned;
- to deliver products which do not meet the intended quality;
- to deliver less than expected;
- to realise fewer benefits than forecast;
- to be cancelled.

Agile development approach controls

It is important to recall that agile development is an approach which exists within the context of a managed project, and that whilst there may be an understandable drive to manage development dynamically, this does not lessen the need to manage the risk of problems or changes along the way. The control cycle remains an underlying foundation, but with techniques that are tuned to reflect the nature of an agile development approach.

Project steering group controls

These are no different to those described earlier and should be applied according to the demands of the Project Steering Group participants and the riskiness of the project itself.

Project manager controls

In addition to any regular progress management activity which the Project Manager considers necessary, there is also the opportunity to manage progress within each iterative cycle; this is one of the great features of agile development. On the assumption that an iteration is of a fixed duration, whoever is charged with the management of the iteration – be that the Project Manager or Iteration Leader – there are four aspects which must be controlled and regulated:

- Effort/cost: There must be sufficient enough resource to deliver the scale and scope of product increment within the iteration. Should progress slip, it may be possible to engage resources in greater number or expertise. Alternatively, a reduction in the scope or quality of what is expected may be negotiated with the Product Owner. This would require an amendment to the Product Backlog to reflect such changes.
- Change: Project-level change may be managed as described earlier, but it may also be co-ordinated at a dynamic level within each iterative cycle. This allows specialists and users to negotiate changes to the emerging product as they work together in harmony. Dependent on the scale of such changes, it may be necessary for the Product Owner to accommodate them in the Product Backlog as items are reappraised and prioritised continuously.
- Quality: In each cycle of development, there is a planned opportunity for users to test the product's emerging quality. This complements any other quality management activity which has been included in the project's governance.
- People: It remains just as important to maintain a motivated team in an agile development environment as it is in any other. Within the daily meeting, the Project Manager or Iteration Leader has a structured opportunity to monitor and maintain their team's enthusiasm for, and commitment to, the work.

A 'daily meeting' was identified in Figure 2.6. At this time-boxed event, team members are encouraged to advise on what they have completed, what they have planned and what barriers may impede their progress. Product quality criteria (as described earlier) may be helpful to clarify what constitutes 'completion'. To maintain the emphasis on dynamism and agility, the meeting commonly takes place standing, often in front of a task board. As illustrated in Figure 9.7, this is a physical, visual representation of those items which are to be started, those which are underway, and those which are complete. It may be referred to as a Scrum task board or Kanban task board, names which reflect the agile development methodologies from which they are taken.

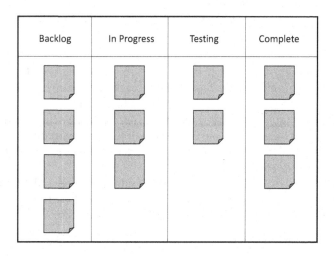

Figure 9.7 Scrum/Kanban task board.

Conclusion

If it is accepted that change is inevitable, it follows that effective controls are needed when progress first begins to diverge from what was planned. Most competent managers delegate, monitor, report and control progress as a matter of course, taking decisions regularly and frequently with little more than their instinct and experience to guide them. However, even the tiniest of changes can have a significant and lasting effect on a project. When added together, a number of small, seemingly insignificant variances can quickly add up to a critical slippage which may affect the underlying justification of the project.

The Project Steering Group and Project Manager can choose how much governance is applied to the project. Their judgement can determine how many of the controls described in this chapter are appropriate for the size, scale and criticality of the project. Too much control, and people in the project will complain of expensive 'micromanagement'. Too little, and the project may fail, one day at a time.

Further reading

Association for Project Management. (2015). *Planning, Scheduling, Monitoring and Control: The Practical Project Management of Time, Cost and Risk*. London, United Kingdom: Association for Project Management.

10 Delivering and closing a project

Abstract

It is best for a project to be initiated according to sound management principles, and this is also true when a project nears its end. This requires progression through a series of steps, one product of which is a Project Closure Report. This captures the status of the project at its recommended point of closure, allowing the Project Steering Group to know the extent to which it has met – or expects to meet – the expectations set out in the Business Case. Whilst acceptance and approval of the Project Closure Report represents an agreement that the project's activities can now come to an end, there remain two further steps to the managed journey of the endeavour and the people who participated in it. First, there is an opportunity to learn lessons which can be used to improve and develop individuals and institutions alike. If an agile approach to development has been applied, lessons may have been continuously identified and accommodated into working practice. Second, if the benefits of the project are yet to accrue at its point of closure, the project's Sponsor can make an assessment some time later to determine whether the intended benefits were actually achieved, and to what extent they outweighed the eventual cost and operation of the project's deliverable.

When, during initiation, people were interested in how long the project would take and what budget it would require, they are now especially interested in the quality of the deliverable which it is due to produce. A managed Closure Stage of a project provides the opportunity for the relevant stakeholders to understand from their individual perspectives what it is delivering, and whether it meets the expectations they set out in the vision. This judgement leads to a point at which they are asked to accept or decline a request to close the project. Certainly, a test or review of some sort may be key in determining the fitness for purpose of the project's principal deliverable. At best, project closure can achieve more than confirmation of the quality of a product. Two other management opportunities present themselves at this time:

- to reflect on lessons that may be learned from the project, and share these with others;
- to prepare for the upcoming post-project period during which the emerging benefits may be measured and realised.

Figure 10.1 focuses on this period in the project lifecycle. Note that these management activities often cannot happen at the same time. Lessons may be learned whilst the project remains fresh in everyone's mind. The assessment of benefits may take place several weeks, months or years after the project has closed, at a point when the benefits are due to have accrued.

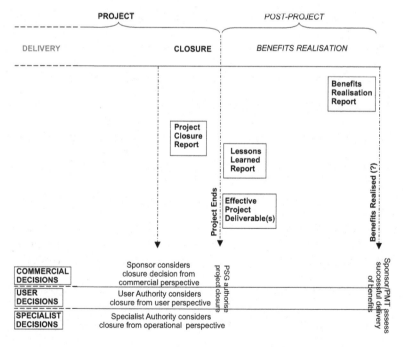

Figure 10.1 Project closure and beyond.

As noted in earlier chapters, this model represents a project which is employing a linear development approach. There are some subtle differences in the closure of a project which has used an agile development approach. These will be described at the end of this chapter.

Project closure

Project Closure is a structured part of the lifecycle which allows for the management environment to be dismantled so that its resources may be freed to engage in work elsewhere. This happens on condition that the Project Steering Group is sufficiently confident to provide their approval to do so.

The Project Manager will be tasked with demonstrating that the project has produced a product to the required standard, within agreed timescales and budgets, and that it has the potential to realise the intended benefits. The Project Steering Group will wish to be clear that it understands whether any work remains outstanding, and what the consequence of that may be.

It is usual for the Project Manager to answer these questions in the form of a report which may be presented to the Project Steering Group. On acceptance of the contents of the report and its recommendation, it may offer its approval. It follows that the Project Closure Report is a key management document which facilitates a crucial decision.

The Project Closure Report

The content of the Project Closure Report may include:

- A list of the documents or statements which serve to describe the baseline against which success will be measured. These may include the Business Case, the Project Plan and the User Requirements Document;
- Some background to describe the project's history. This may be helpful in identifying any anomalies (such as changes) which have led to variances or course diversions;
- A detailed review of how the actual performance of the project compares to the baseline;
- Matters outstanding, such as:
  - any products which have been delivered in addition to those identified in the plan;
  - any products which were planned but not delivered;

- any benefits which have been identified in addition to those originally included in the Business Case;
- any benefits which have been removed or reduced in value;
- a list of change requests and issues, identifying their status at the point of closure, specifically noting any which have been declined or deferred until a later release;

- a description of the management environment which is to be put in place to govern the period after the project has closed, leading towards and including the final measurement of realised benefits;
- options for the Project Steering Group to consider. Note that there may be alternatives to a straightforward decision to close the project, including the postponement of some part of the project's scope to a supplementary stage;
- a recommendation and plan to articulate the Project Manager's preferred and proposed course of action.

In drawing together the evidence needed to facilitate an effective closure decision – and approval to move into the post-project benefits realisation stage – the Project Manager may review the Project Closure Report against the following criteria:

- Is there sufficient information for the Project Steering Group to close the project with confidence?
- Is there evidence of the extent to which expectations of success outlined at the start of the project have been met?
- Is the information used both accurate and current?
- Is there a plan to show what must happen during the Benefits Realisation period, and how it is to be governed?
- Are the roles and responsibilities of those involved in the measurement and realisation of benefits clearly and commonly understood?

Closing the project

Having gathered knowledge of the state of the project at its proposed point of closure – and captured this in the Project Closure Report – the Project Manager can ensure the operational readiness of the project's product, and facilitate the Project Steering Group's decision-making. This may involve:

- completing all tests and securing evidence of their successful outcome;
- where necessary, gaining agreement from the specialists that they have what they need to support the product after project closure;

- putting in place procedures in the event that it becomes necessary to reverse the release of the deliverable into the operational environment;
- arranging a meeting for the Project Steering Group to consider the Project Closure Report and, if acceptable, approve the closure of the project, signifying that:
- no further investment will be made in the project and no further costs should be committed to project cost codes;
- project team members have been informed of the closure and their line managers instructed to seek new engagements for them;
- a 'lessons learned' review may be scheduled and funded to allow for the participation of all relevant project stakeholders;
- the User Authorities and Specialist Authorities will be held accountable for ensuring that the project's product is adopted, maintained and operated in the 'business-as-usual' environment;
- the post-project period is beginning and that the Sponsor (or other approved individual) will be held accountable to ensure that the intended benefits are realised.

The post-project period

Learning lessons

A 'lessons learned' review offers an opportunity to reflect on the way in which the project was managed. A successful review depends on:

- the involvement of representatives of all levels of management and leadership;
- being conducted near enough to the end of the project so that observations are clear and accurate;
- both positive and negative aspects of project management being given sufficient consideration;
- the identification of – and commitment to – clear improvement actions;
- clear and timely measures of success for each action.

The lessons learned review

The experience of the project needs to remain fresh in people's minds for the review to be effective. Any of the project's stakeholders may be invited, especially including the leadership and management team members. It is an opportunity not only to contribute, but to learn from experience because, in this way, improvements may be shared across the institution.

As the audience may be diverse and, occasionally, emotional, external facilitation can be helpful. Here is a simple agenda:

- Introduction: the Sponsor lends their authority to the review;
- Ground rules: acknowledging that the review may become emotional, the following guidelines may help to keep the review focused:
  - park issues;
  - work within the agenda;
  - respect the facilitator;
  - prepare in advance;
  - do not criticise individuals;
  - speak one at a time;
  - make observations clearly, once and politely.
- Observations: a set of starter questions may be used to encourage and inspire an exploration of the subject areas, identifying and highlighting those which the group considers most deserving of attention;
- Break: an opportunity for participants to leave behind what may have been an emotionally charged session in readiness for the next, which is intended to be focused on improvements;
- Lessons learned: participants focus on the highlighted observations, identifying ways of overcoming the issues, and doing more of what was considered to be positive.
- Action plan: to make clear what the action entails, how its completion will be measured, who is responsible for completing it and by when, taking care to assign actions only to those who have participated in the review.

The lessons learned report

The report is a product of the review. It is likely to reflect the review's agenda and structure:

- Project background: a brief outline of the project itself for readers who may not be familiar with it, or who were unable to participate in the review;
- Objectives: to describe the purpose of the review, typically:
  - to make a contribution to the continued development and improvement of the management of the organisation's projects;

- to provide an opportunity for colleagues to express their opinions.
- Scope: how widely is the management of the project being reviewed? What exclusions are there, if any? Areas of investigation may include:
  - the project's organisation, including management roles and responsibilities;
  - communications and the management of stakeholders;
  - planning and delegation;
  - monitoring, reporting and control;
  - change control;
  - quality management, including the specification, build, testing and approval of products;
  - the management of risk.
- Observations: what observations did the participants identify? This section should include a consideration of both good and poor habits.
- Lessons learned: in conclusion, what lessons can be learned from those observations?
- Action plan: how will the lessons be implemented?

The benefits realisation review

As the Sponsor is to be held accountable for the return on the investment made in the project, their responsibilities are not complete until a review has taken place to determine the extent to which the planned benefits have been realised. The cost/benefit assessment in the Business Case will have determined when those benefits are due to have accrued. Therefore, when that moment arrives, it will be possible to conduct a Benefits Realisation Review.

This requires that accrued benefits and costs are compared. The costs at this point will include both project-spend and the subsequent costs of operating the project's product. It is to be hoped that the comparison determines a successful commercial outcome, as forecast. If, however, the outcome is not as expected, the Sponsor has the opportunity during the benefits realisation period to take further corrective action.

It can be helpful to produce a report whenever a Benefits Realisation Review is undertaken so that the results may be shared, and for actions to be agreed. Commonly, the contents may include:

- Summary: recording the actual and forecast operational spend and benefits realised, identifying variances and escalation conditions;

- Variances: an analysis of the key discrepancies between planned and actual benefits;
- Corrective actions: a description of what will be done by whom to address the variances;
- Changes to governance: a narrative section to determine what, if anything, must be done to change the governance of the Benefits Realisation period in order to increase the likelihood of success;
- Conclusion: to provide an opportunity for the Sponsor to summarise the outcome of the review;
- Recommendations to allow the Sponsor to propose how the Benefits Realisation period should continue, if at all.

Closure when applying an agile development approach

The agile manifesto asserts that 'regularly, the team reflects on how to become more effective, and adjusts accordingly'. The 'retrospective' is a management discipline which may be exercised within each iterative cycle, and is a planned opportunity for the team to learn and apply lessons from the recent development iteration. Given the agile manifesto's focus on pace, reduced scope and much less paperwork, a retrospective may be brief – perhaps no more than 45 minutes long – and undocumented. Practically, it poses the same questions as the lessons learned review described earlier:

- What went well?
- What did not?
- What improvements may be made?

A project containing some agile development will have the opportunity to deploy releases of features or functionality throughout the life of the project. Whilst each release may be smaller in scope than that which appears at the close of a more traditional, linear project, similar care and attention must be accorded to each. This is because every deployment represents a transference from the project to the organisation of some new products or services which will impact it in some way. Each has the potential to drive – or require – a change in working practices or behaviours.

As for any project, 'closure' provides a managed opportunity to remove the project's management governance. When the Project Steering Group is asked to approve the project's closure, the Product Owner should pay special attention to the condition of the Product Backlog, the Product Roadmap and the Product Vision. This will provide an opportunity to determine the extent to which the items anticipated for inclusion have been delivered within the constraints of time and money available. In a dynamic environment, further increments may be discussed or encouraged. This should take place within a continued commitment to manage any further development within the governance of a project, and within the context of an organisation that may have plenty else in which it wishes to invest its scarce resources.

Finally, whilst the incremental release of a product's or service's features may have released some value during the life of the project, the benefits of the entire project must be assessed at some point after its closure. This will determine the extent to which the investment was sensible, and that any changes in working practices or behaviours are now happening as a second nature.

Conclusion

Much of a project's success depends on an effective working partnership between a Project Manager and their Sponsor. The Project Manager's responsibilities have strict limits within the life of the project, and are curtailed at the point of closure. They may have employed the best and most suitable principles and techniques to the management of the project, hopefully meeting expectations of a timely, fit-for-purpose delivery which is on budget. However, impressive as they may seem, the mere delivery of new systems, processes, products and services does not cause change to take place; it merely facilitates it. The leader of the change – the Project Sponsor – must remain committed to embedding new behaviours which release the benefits. If such changes are not adopted, the project may not be considered a success, despite what it may appear to have delivered. Therefore, it is the Sponsor, on behalf of the organisation which funded the project, who is ultimately accountable for delivering lasting benefit through the effective management of change.

Further reading

Bradley, Gerald. (2016). *Benefit Realisation Management: A Practical Guide for Achieving Benefits through Change*. Oxford, United Kingdom: Routledge.

11 The absolutely essential 'absolute essentials'

For those who have a practical interest in the management of projects, it is helpful to think of principles, techniques and tools identified in this book as ways of addressing the risks that these endeavours bring with them. The amount of management used in a project should be proportionate to the amount of risk it faces. With this in mind, here is a simple summary of the ways in which the project's leaders and managers may address that risk.

- Know who the project's stakeholders are, and which of them should be inside (and outside) the project's management team (see Chapter 3):
  - compile a Stakeholder Matrix to better understand the 'people landscape';
  - develop an Organisation Chart which is suited to the project;
  - design and implement a strong and reliable Project Steering Group to own and direct the project. The participants should be:
    - authoritative;
    - experienced;
    - balanced as a group to reflect the competing commercial, user and specialist interests;
    - led by a strong and committed Sponsor.
  - for projects pursuing an agile development approach, include the Product Owner.
  - engage a Project Manager who has the capability to plan, monitor and control time, cost and quality.
- Know what 'success' looks like from each of the three competing commercial, user and specialist perspectives (see Chapter 4). Describe those expectations in the form of:

- a cost/benefit analysis, embedded in the heart of the Business Case, where the costs and benefits are compared to determine the likely advantages of the change being sought;
- other success criteria, also contained in the Business Case, but representing the measures which will be used by the User Authorities and Specialist Authorities to describe their aspirations;
- the Product Vision and Product Roadmap (for projects pursuing an agile development approach).
- Know how the Project Steering Group's expectations are to be met:
  - apply a product-based approach to planning in order to determine what deliverables will be needed to meet the Project Steering Group's expectations (see Chapter 5);
  - identify the resources which will be needed to develop and deliver those products;
  - estimate the time needed during which those resources may be employed;
  - refine the plan and seek compromise where necessary;
  - create a Project Plan which draws together the time, cost and quality plans (see Chapter 6);
  - utilise a combination of product or service development approaches according to the needs of the project;
  - outline and agree on the controls which will be used to keep the project on track, especially escalation criteria (see Chapter 8).
- Know the risks, and how to manage them (see Chapter 7):
  - use a process to support a risk-aware mindset;
  - seek to identify those things which may impact the project;
  - determine which require management and put in place mitigating actions;
  - ensure that these actions are carried out;
  - use the Risk Register as a record.
- Initiate the project under controlled conditions (see Chapter 8):
  - answer the five essential questions in the Business Case and Project Governance Report:
    - *Who* needs to be involved in the management of the project?
    - *What* must the project deliver?
    - *When* must it deliver?
    - *How* much must be invested?
    - *Why* is this project necessary?
  - allow the project to progress *only* on the instruction of the Project Steering Group.

- Control the project's progress (see Chapter 9):
  - control what has been planned:
    - time
    - budget
    - quality
    - risks
    - benefits
  - use Project Forecast Reports to identify where variances have occurred and instigate corrective action where it is needed;
  - use escalation criteria to identify the extent of variances, allowing the Project Steering Group to be engaged if/when the project demands greater authority than is present in the Project Manager;
  - use quality reviews to ensure the project produces deliverables of the expected standard;
  - use change control to understand and manage the consequences of issues and change requests;
  - for projects pursuing an agile development approach, embed quality and change controls within each iterative cycle.
- Use structured project closure techniques to gain the formal commitment needed to close the project (see Chapter 10):
  - describe the state of the project at the point of closure in the Project Closure Report, and seek its formal approval by the Project Steering Group;
  - learn from the experience and share that learning with the wider organisation wherever possible (this may be achieved during the life of the project, especially where an agile development approach is being applied);
  - measure realised benefits to determine the extent to which the project succeeded.

Any intervention which limits the likelihood or impact of a risk to the project's management and leadership, increases its chances of success. This is an aspiration which we might all agree is absolutely essential.

Appendix A – Case studies

The following news reports describe some of the difficulties faced in managing complex projects. However, the challenges faced may have been addressed with the application of principles and techniques described in this book.

Having read the articles, describe what risks may have been addressed in advance to mitigate some of the issues which developed.

Case summary	Hyperlink	Industry/region
Berlin Brandenburg: the airport with half a million faults. A BBC news article describing the challenges of managing a project in an ever-changing world.	https://www.bbc.co.uk/ news/world-48527308	Construction/ World
'Failed' borders scheme. A BBC news article about the delays and budget-overruns experienced whilst implementing an e-borders' scheme.	https://www.bbc.co.uk/ news/uk-34988913	Information Technology/ UK

Further classroom exercises are available online.

Index

Note: **Bold** page numbers refer to tables and *italic* page numbers refer to figures.

absolute essentials, project
    management 120–122
activity network *62*, 62–65
actual to date (ATD) 100
agile project development approach
    79; control cycle 108–109, *110*;
    Gantt chart *67*; hierarchy
    of management 26–27, *27*;
    principles 13; project closure
    118–119; values 12
agile project development lifecycle 35;
    planning quality 46–50
assumption, risks 74
audience *45*, 46
avoidance, risks 75

baseline 86
benefits, project 31–32; balanced
    decision-making 21; commercial
    quantification 8–9; cost/benefit
    analysis 33–34, **34**; generation
    7, 7–8; incremental 35–36;
    quantifying **32**, 32–33; returns
    delivering stage 9–12; *vs.* cost
    6, 6–7
benefits realisation review 117–118
bottom-up estimation 54, *54*
budget 4, 15, 17, 31, 40, 55, 72, 75, 95,
    96, 99, *101*, 101, 103, 105, 107, 113
'business-as-usual' (BAU) 3–4
business case 33, 36, 37, 99–100, 102;
    interdependencies 82; opportunity/
    problem 82; options to address the

problem 83; selected option 83–84;
    strategic fit 82; success, commercial
    measures 82–83

change control 104–107, 106
characteristics, project: budget 4;
    change lifecycle 4–5, *5*; defined
    end date 4; lifecycle 4–5, *5*;
    people involvement 4; produces
    a deliverable 3–4; resources 4;
    successful project 5–6
commercial success, project:
    benefits 31–32; comparison of
    35; cost/benefit analysis 33–34,
    34; incremental benefits 35–36;
    quantified benefits **32**, 32–33;
    sponsor's interest 30–31; summarised
    costs **33**; value of money **34**, 34–35
contingency, risks 75, 77
control cycle: agile development
    approach 108–109, *110*; delegation
    of work 95–96; monitor, report
    and control (*see* monitor, report
    and control mechanisms); plan 95;
    progress management 92–93, *93*
corrective action 107–108
cost/benefit analysis 33–34, **34**
costs estimation, projects:
    comparison of 35; cost/benefit
    analysis 33–34, **34**; generation
    7, 7–8; summarised **33**; value of
    money **34**, 34–35; *vs.* benefits *6*, 6–7
critical path analysis 63, *63*

delegation 27, 95–96
deliverables 3–4, 14, 15, 17, 29, *31*, 40, 42, 47, 50, 51, *57*, 79, 81, 84, 87, 95, *101*, 111, 112, 121, 122
Delphi technique, estimation 55
dependencies 42, 43, 47, 59, 62, 70, 71, 81, 82, 87
derivation, product *45*, 46
discounted cash flow **34**, 34–35
duration (DUR) 63, *63*

earliest finish time (EFT) 63, 63
earliest start time (EST) 63, *63*
earned value analysis 102–103
effort and duration, estimation 59, *60*
end date 4, 62, 63, 94, 99, 100, 107
estimate, project: bottom-up 54, *54*; definition 53; Delphi technique 55; effort and duration 59, *60*; estimating sheet **58**, 58–59; Gantt chart 59, *60*; productivity of people 56–57; resource plan 60, **61**; standard project/product 56, *56*; top-down 53–54, *54*; trustworthiness 57; work distribution 55, *55*
estimate to complete (ETC) 100
estimating sheet **58**, 58–59
evaluation, risks 73, *74*

float 63, *63*, 64
forecast at completion (FAC) 100

Gantt chart 59, *60, 67, 68*

Herzberg, F. 56–57
hierarchy of management: agile development approach 26–27, *27*; organisation structure *22*; portfolio management team 23; project manager 24–25; project steering group 23–24

identification, risks 71–72
impact, risk *73*; lessen 74
incremental project development approach 10, *12*, 81–82
initiation, project: business case 82–84; incremental development approach 81–82; linear 79–81; project governance report 84–91

internal rate of return (IRR) 35
issues 9, 70, 71, 73, 75, 91, 102, 106, *106*, 114, 116, 123
iterative project development approach 10, *11*, 47, 50

latest finish time (LFT) 63, *63*
latest start time (LST) 63, *63*
leadership, and management 18–19
lessening the impact, risks 74
lessons learned: report 116–117; review 115–116
likelihood 72–73; scale of *73*

management by exception 93–95
managing complex projects, challenges faced 123
milestones 17, 40, 65, 100
mitigation, risks 74–75
monitor, report and control mechanisms: change control 104–107, *106*; corrective action 107–108; project manager 98–108; project steering group 96–98

net present value (NPV) 35

organisation: communications plan 85–86; roles and responsibilities 85; structure of 85

plan: building 52–61; incremental delivery 66, *67*, 68, *68*; refining 62–66
planning quality: agile lifecycle 46–50; failure to focus on products 39; plan components 40; product-based approach 40–46
portfolio 15
portfolio management team 23, 79–80
portfolio/programme office 25
PRINCE project management methodology 41, 74, 84–85
product backlog 10, 26, 47, 50, 66, 68, 79, 81, 109
product-based planning approach: activity *vs.* product 41; product breakdown structure 42–43, *43, 48*; product, definition 40; product description 44–46, *45*; product flow diagram 43–44, *44, 49*

product breakdown structure 42–43, *43, 48*
product description 44–46, *45*
product flow diagram 43–44, *44, 49,* 57, *57*
product owner 26, 36, 47
product roadmap 36, 47, 68, 121
product vision 36, 47
productivity 56–61, 107, 108
programme 16
progress management 92–93
project: benefits outweighs the investment 15; definition 14–15; produces a specified deliverable 15; temporary management environment 15; *vs.* portfolio 15; *vs.* programme 16
project benefit forecast 102
project closure: agile development approach 118–119; benefits realisation review 117–118; management activities 111–112, *112*; operational readiness, project 114–115; project closure report 113–114; report 113–114
project development approaches: agile (*see* agile project development approach); deciding the suitable approach 13–14; incremental 10, *12*, 81–82; iterative 10, *11*, 47, 50
project evaluation review technique *65*, 65–66
project forecast report: actual to date 100; baseline 99–100; benefit forecast 102; budget forecast 101, *101*; definition 99; earned value analysis 102–103; estimate to complete 100; forecast at completion 100; quality forecast *101*, 101–102; quality review 104, *105*; risks and issues 102; time forecast 100, *101*; variance 100
project governance report 94, 100; organisation 85–86; plan 86–91
project initiation: structured 79
project lifecycle 4–5, 81–82, 93, 97, 112
project management: absolute essentials 120–122; budget 17; definition 16; deliverables 17; people involved 16–17; project

objectives 17; *see also individual entries*
project manager 1; activity network 62, 62–65; change control 104–107, *106*; corrective action 107–108; emerging project team, planning 42; failure to focus on products 39; float and planning flexibility 63, *63*, 64; hierarchy of management 24–25; organisational design 22; plan building 52–53; principal responsibility 98; product breakdown structure 42–43, *43*; product flow diagram 43–44, *44*; project closure report 113–114; Project Forecast Report 99–104; relationship with Project Steering Group 94; resource levelling *64*, 64–65; risk register 75, **76**; team progress meeting 98–99; understanding perspectives 37
project office 25–26
project organisational design, principles of: balanced decision-making 21; existence within the organisation 20–21; organisation structure 22; single project manager 22
project outline 79–80
project plan 24, 39–40, 53, 79; change control 90; configuration control 90; control 89; documentary/procedural standards 88; meetings and reporting 89; planning 88; quality 87; quality control 90–91; resource plan 88; responsibilities and accountability 87; risks 88–89; time schedule 88; understanding the deliverables 87; variance 89–90
project steering group 71, 113–115; hierarchy of management 23–24; plan building 52–53; project lifecycle and change success 29–30, *30*; project plan 86; relationship with project manager 94; scheduled stage meetings 97; understanding perspectives 37; unscheduled project steering group meeting 97–98

project success, defining principles:
    commercial 30–36, *31*; specialist
    31, 36–37; understanding
    perspectives 37; user *31*, 36

qualification, risks 72–73
quality: criteria *45*, 46, 47; forecast
    101, 101–102; method *45*, 46;
    planning (*see* planning quality);
    review 104, *105*

reaction to change, anticipating
    18–19, *19*
red, amber and green (RAG)
    reporting 95
refining, project plan: activity
    network *62*, 62–65; critical path
    analysis 63, *63*; project evaluation
    review technique *65*, 65–66;
    resource levelling *64*, 64–65; tuning
    64, *64*
reporting 17, 25, 89, 95, 96–98,
    101, 103
resource levelling *64*, 64–65
resource plan 17, 59, 60, **61**, 64, 65,
    88, 96
resources 4, 10, 15, 18, 23, 24, 25, 35,
    40, 41, 53, 58, 65, 66, 74, 79, 86, 88,
    97, 101, 107, 109, 121
responsibilities 20–28, 47, 85, 87, 95,
    98, 117, 119
revenue 32, **32**, 33, 101
risk factor 73, *74*
risk management: challenges faced,
    managing complex projects 123;
    principles 70–71; process of *71*,
    71–75
risk matrix *72*
risk register 75, **76**
risks, assumptions, issues and
    dependencies (RAID) 70–71

Scrum task board/Kanban task
    board 109, *110*
selected option, business case:
    benefits 83; benefits realisation

plan 84; cost/benefit analysis 84;
    costs 83–84; deliverables and
    timescales 84; planning 84; risks 83
sharing burden/cost, risks 75
solution design document 81, 91
specialist authorities 23, 29, 81,
    115, 121
specialist success *31*, 36–37
Specific, Measurable, Achievable,
    Realistic and Timely (SMART)
    approach 37
sponsor 1, 29, 79–81, 119; balancing
    project cost and rewards 36;
    understanding perspectives 37
stage 9, 54, 55, 79, 80, 85, 91, 92, 111,
    114; meetings 97; plans 53–54
stakeholders 16–17
standard project/product estimation
    56, *56*
successful project characteristics 5–6

tasks 52
team progress meeting 98, *98*
terms of reference 96
time forecast 100, *101*
timescales and budgets planning:
    incremental delivery 66, *67*, 68, *68*;
    plan building 52–61; refining plan
    62–66
top-down estimation 53–54, *54*

unscheduled project steering group
    meeting 97–98
updated product backlog 47
US Department of Defence 65
user authorities 23, 29, 36, 115, 121
user requirements document *31*,
    36, 81
user success *31*, 36

variance 100

waterfall project development
    approach 10, *11*
work distribution, estimation 55, *55*
work-stream leaders 25

Printed in the United States
by Baker & Taylor Publisher Services